Hidden Images:
Symbolism of the Heart
Coloring Book

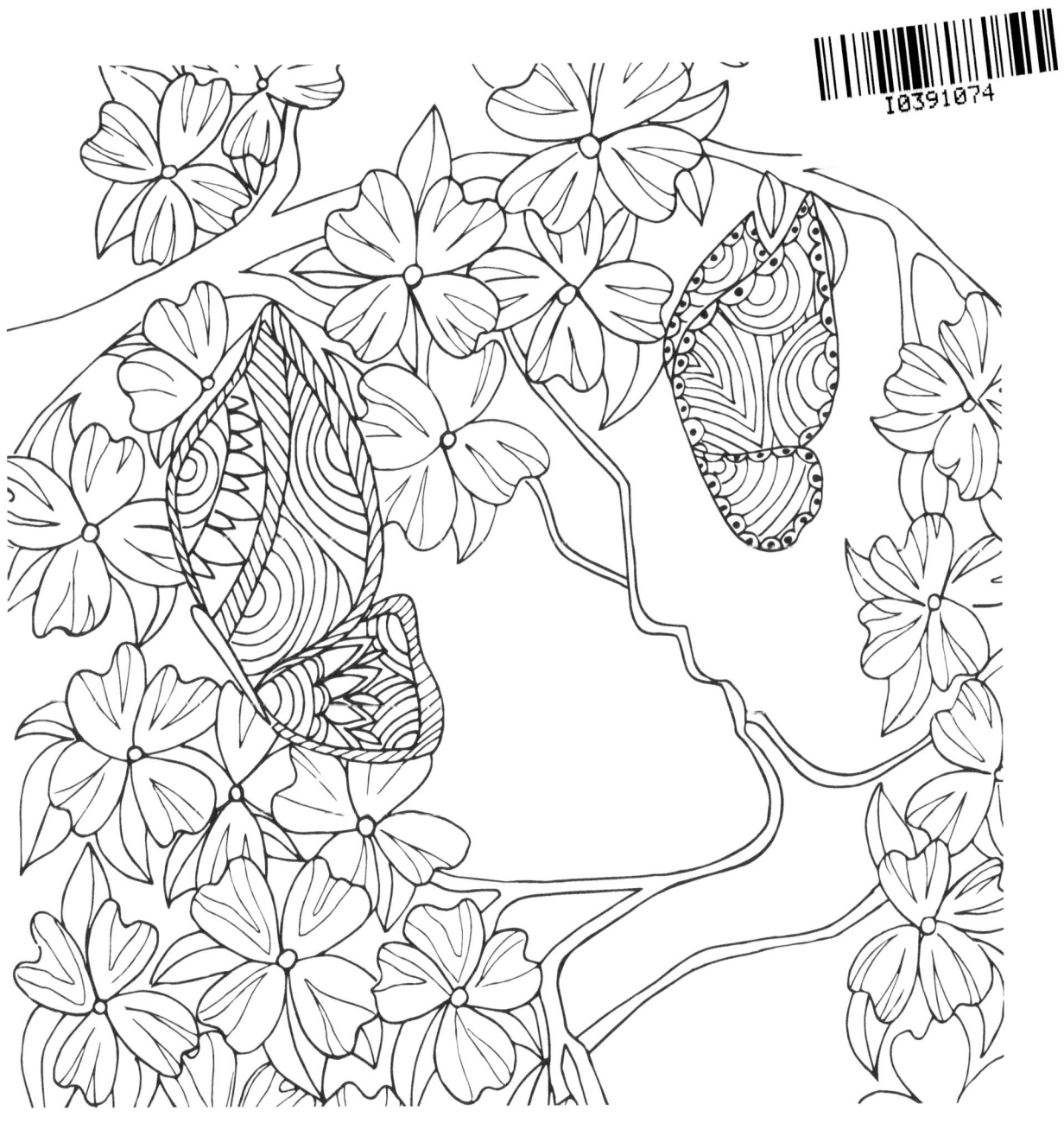

Serena Daugette

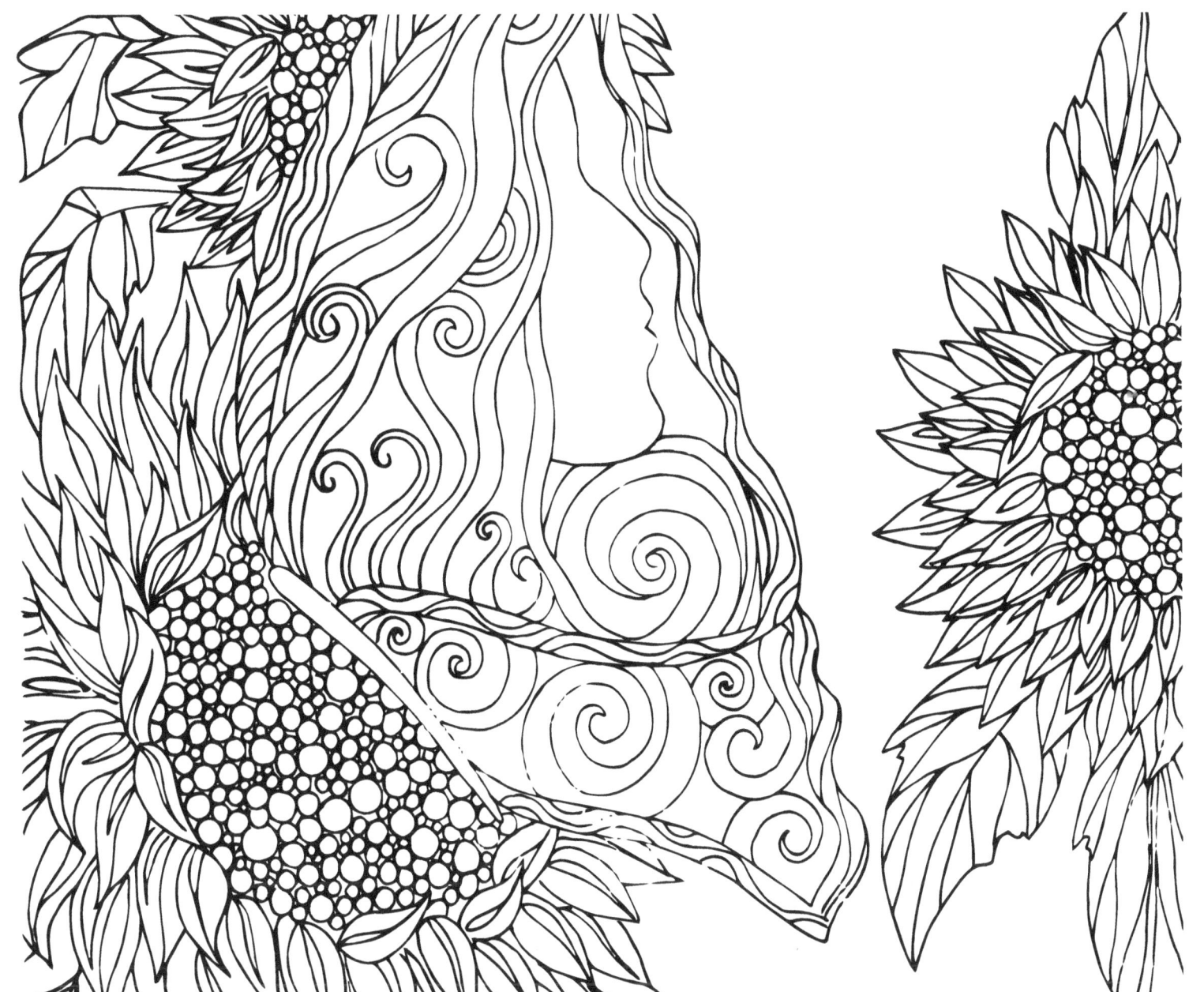

Printed by CreateSpace

International Standard Book Number
ISBN-13: 978-1541118805
ISBN-10: 1541118804

Available from Amazon.com, CreateSpace.com,
and other retail outlets.

www.CreateSpace.com/HiddenImages

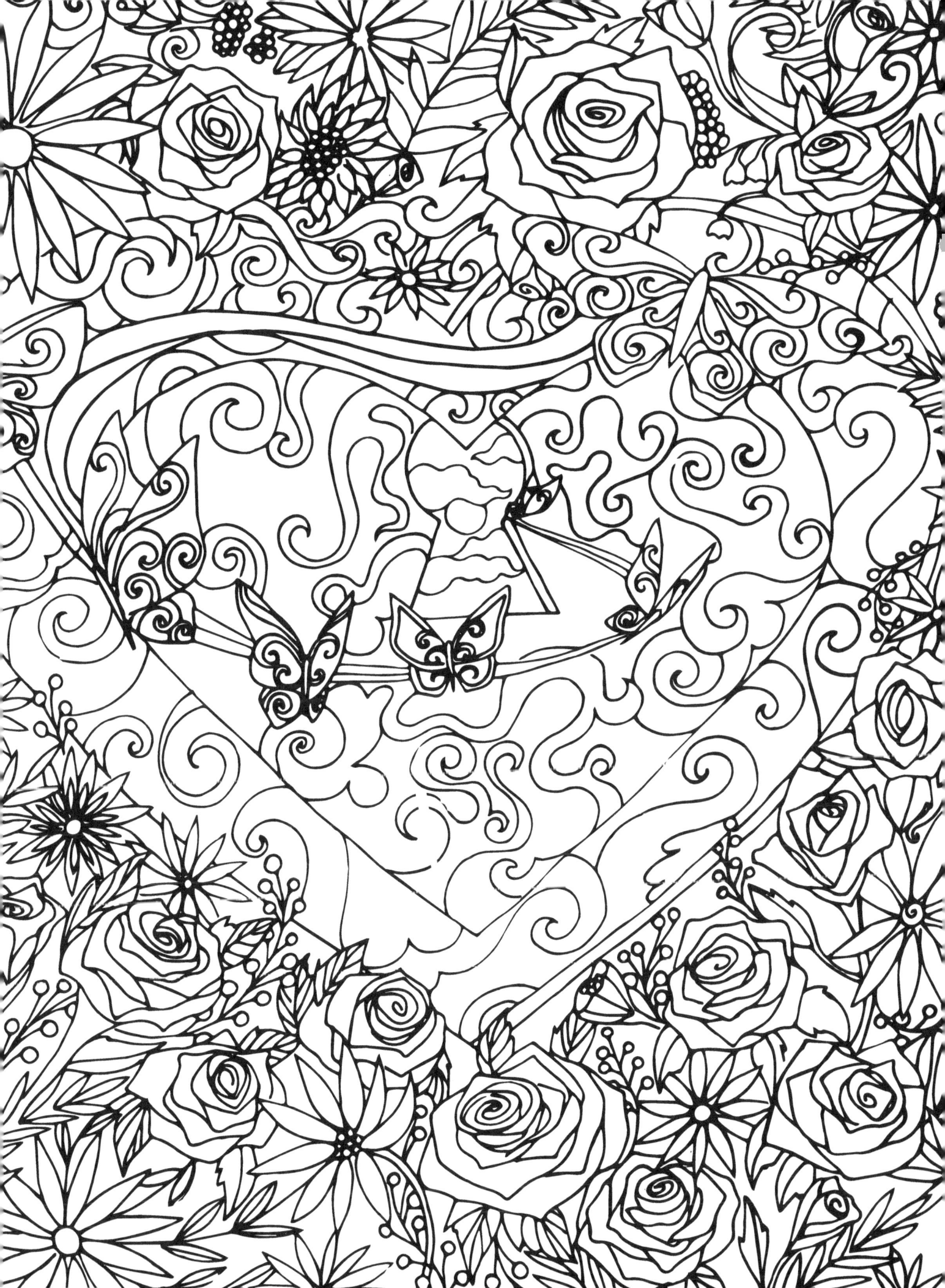

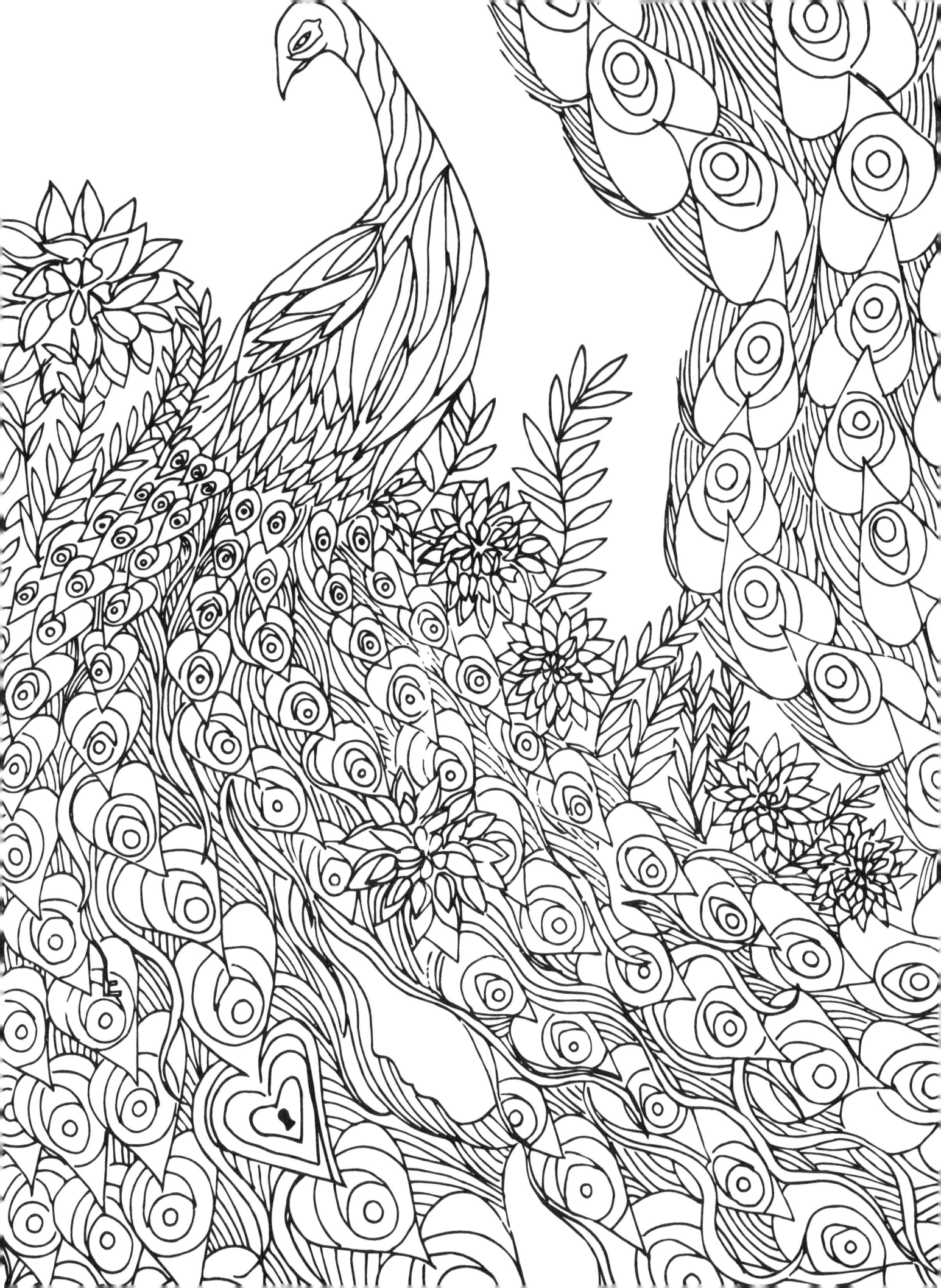

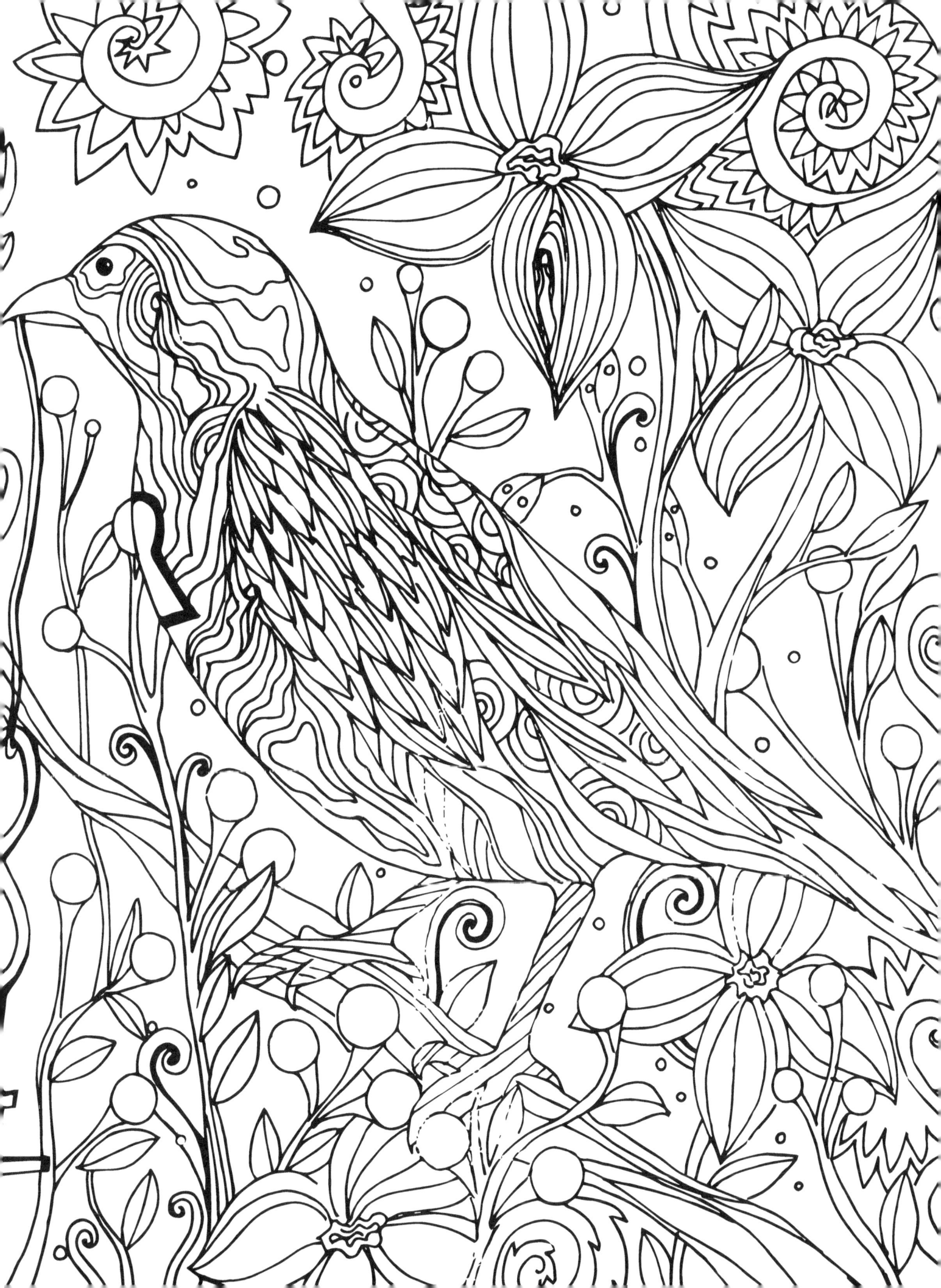

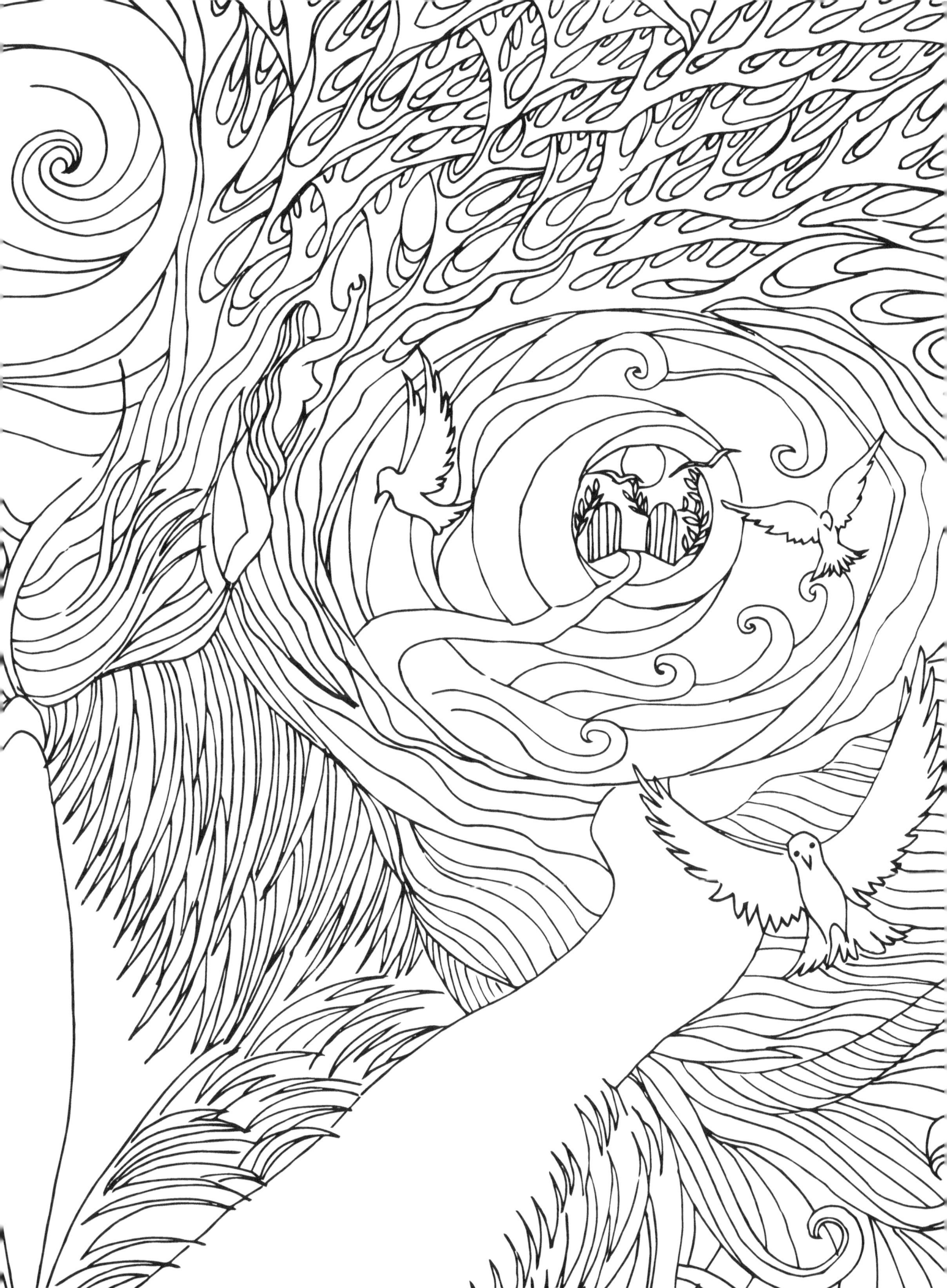

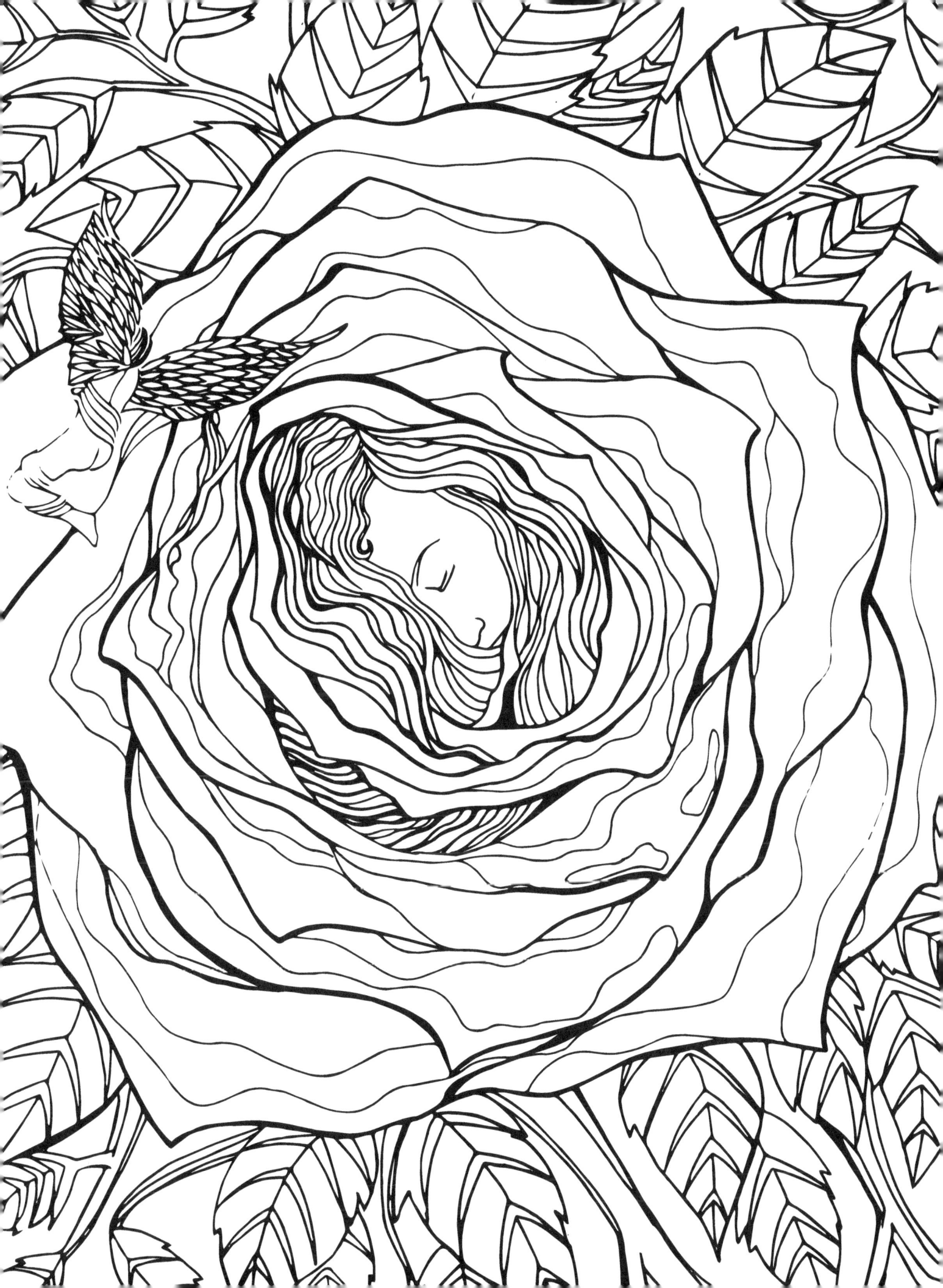

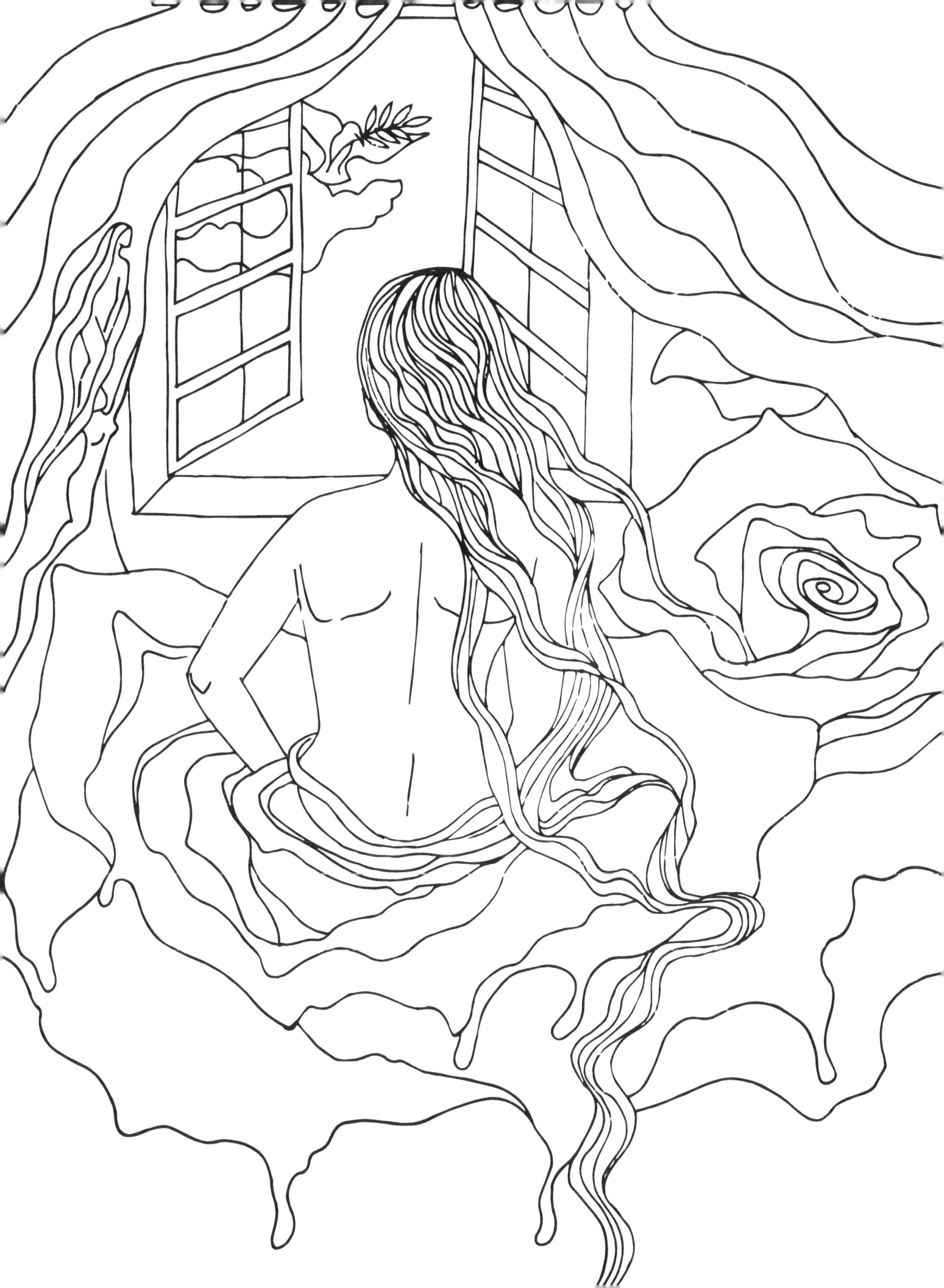

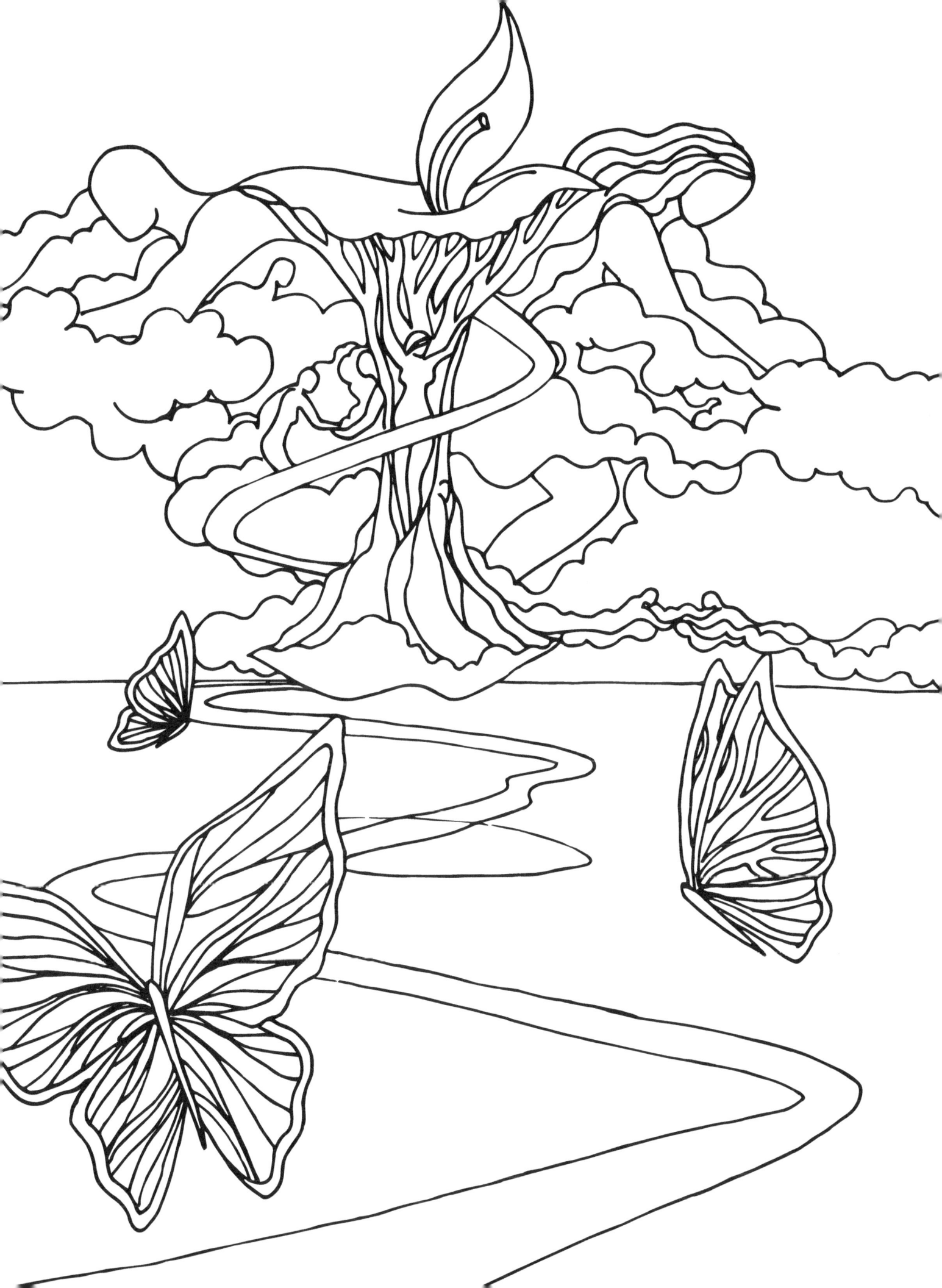

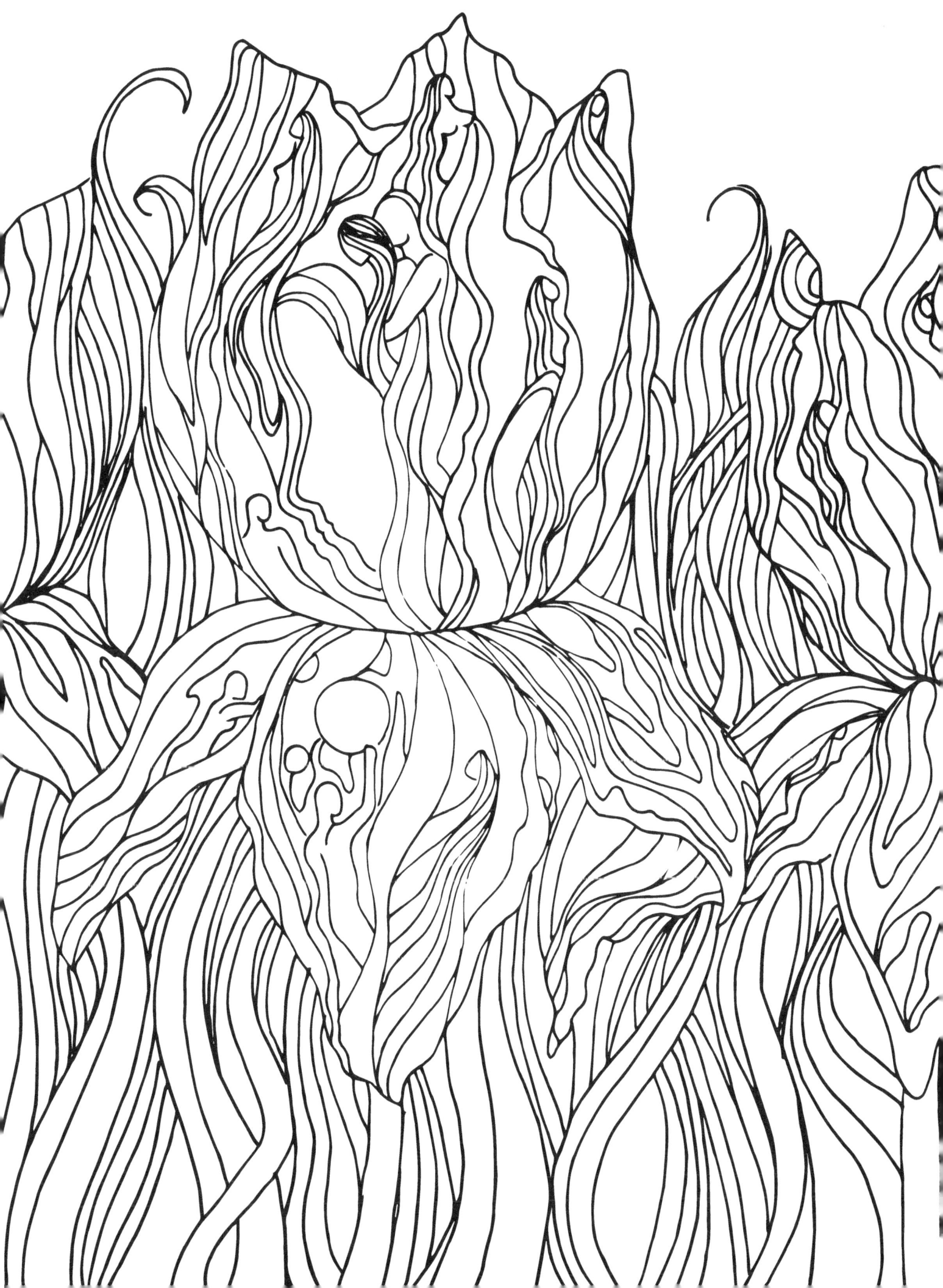

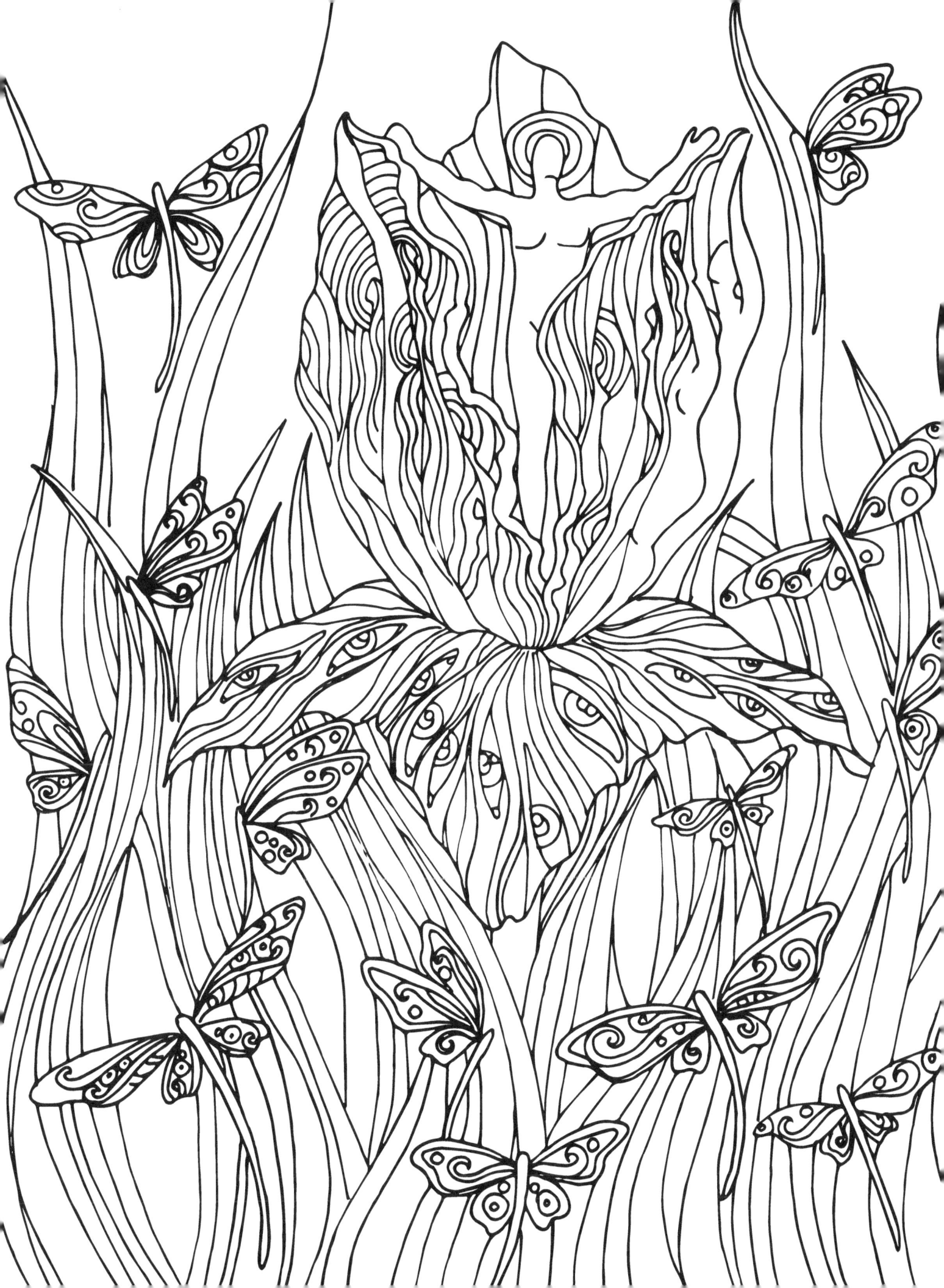

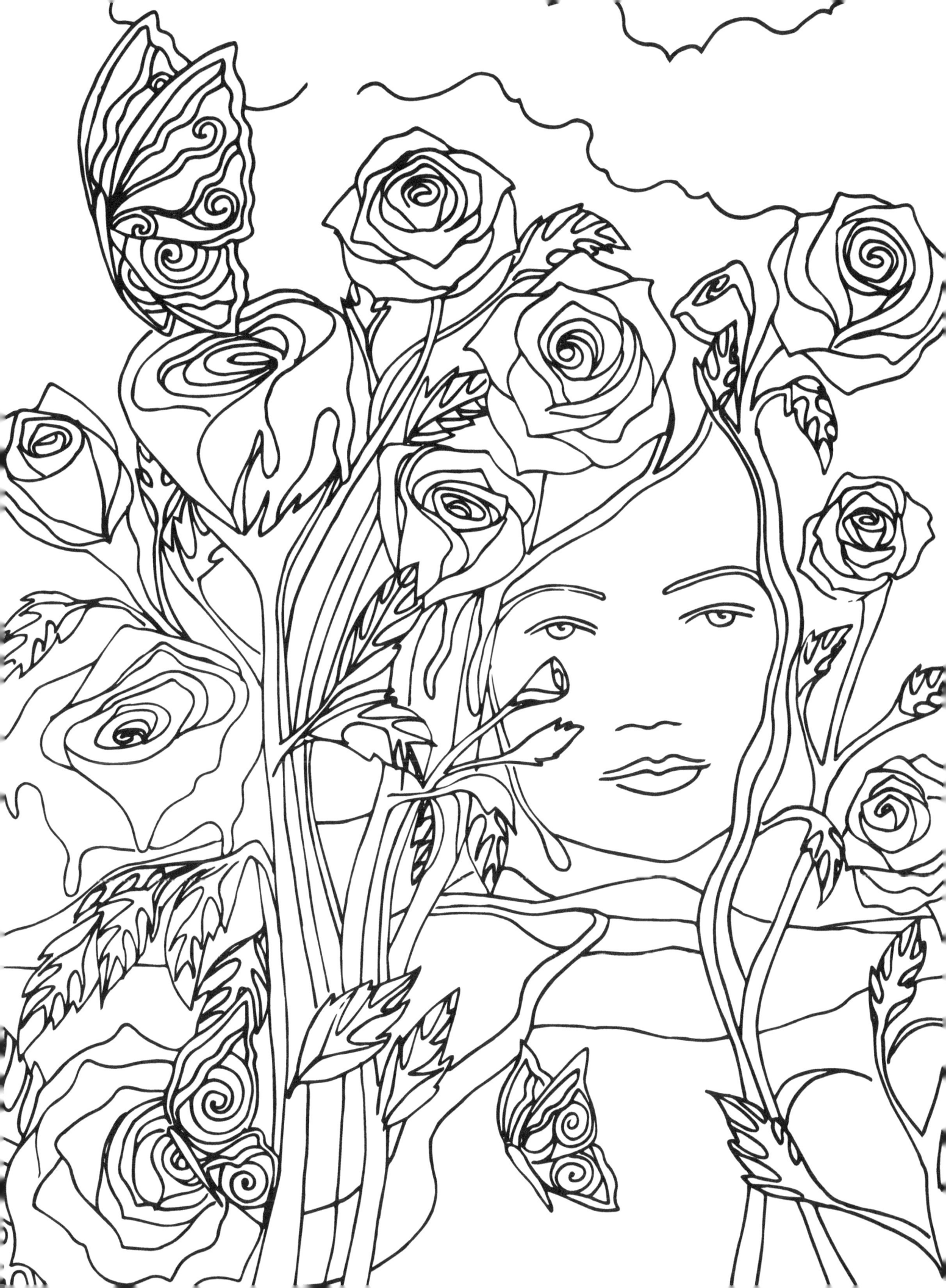

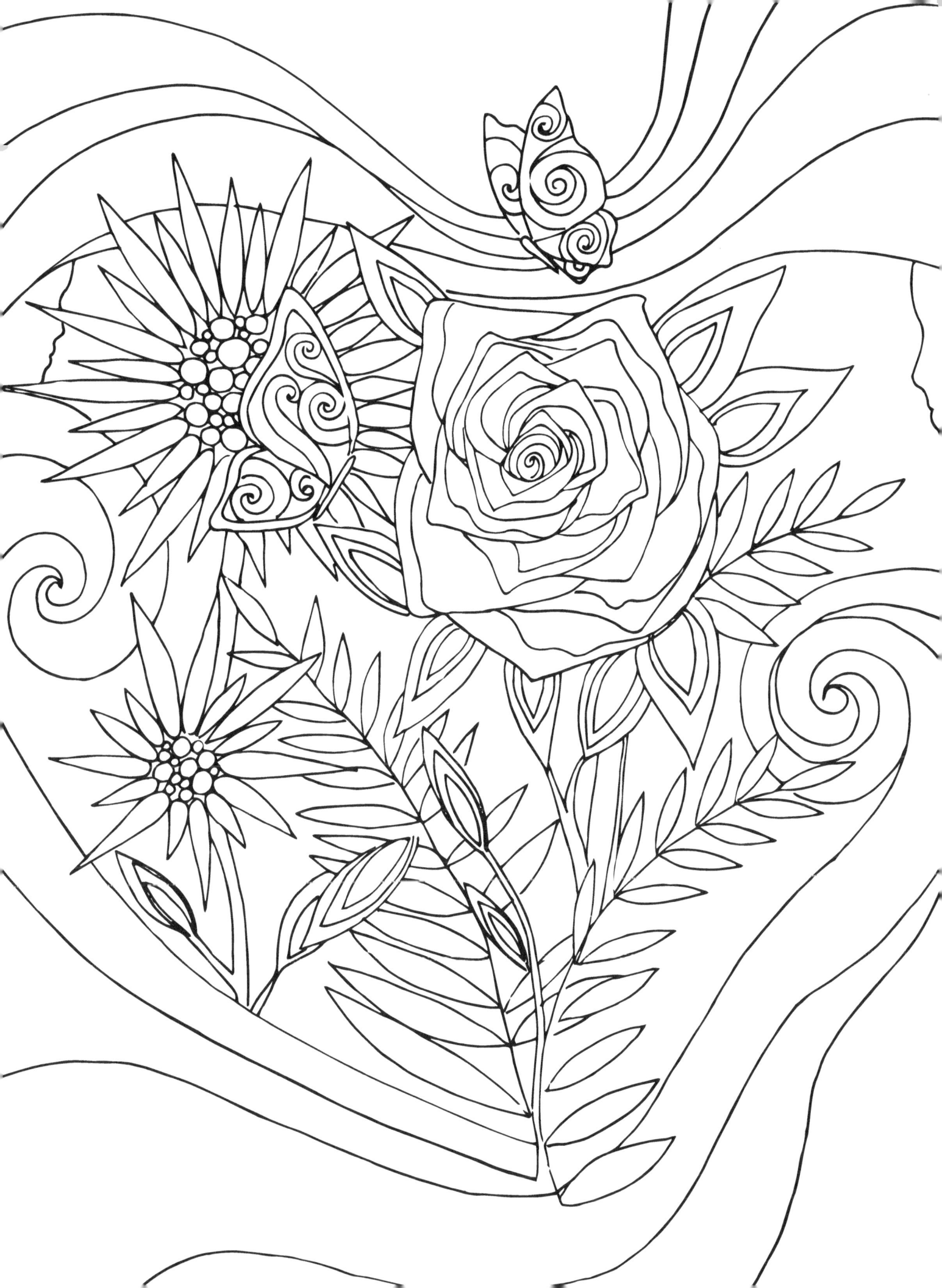

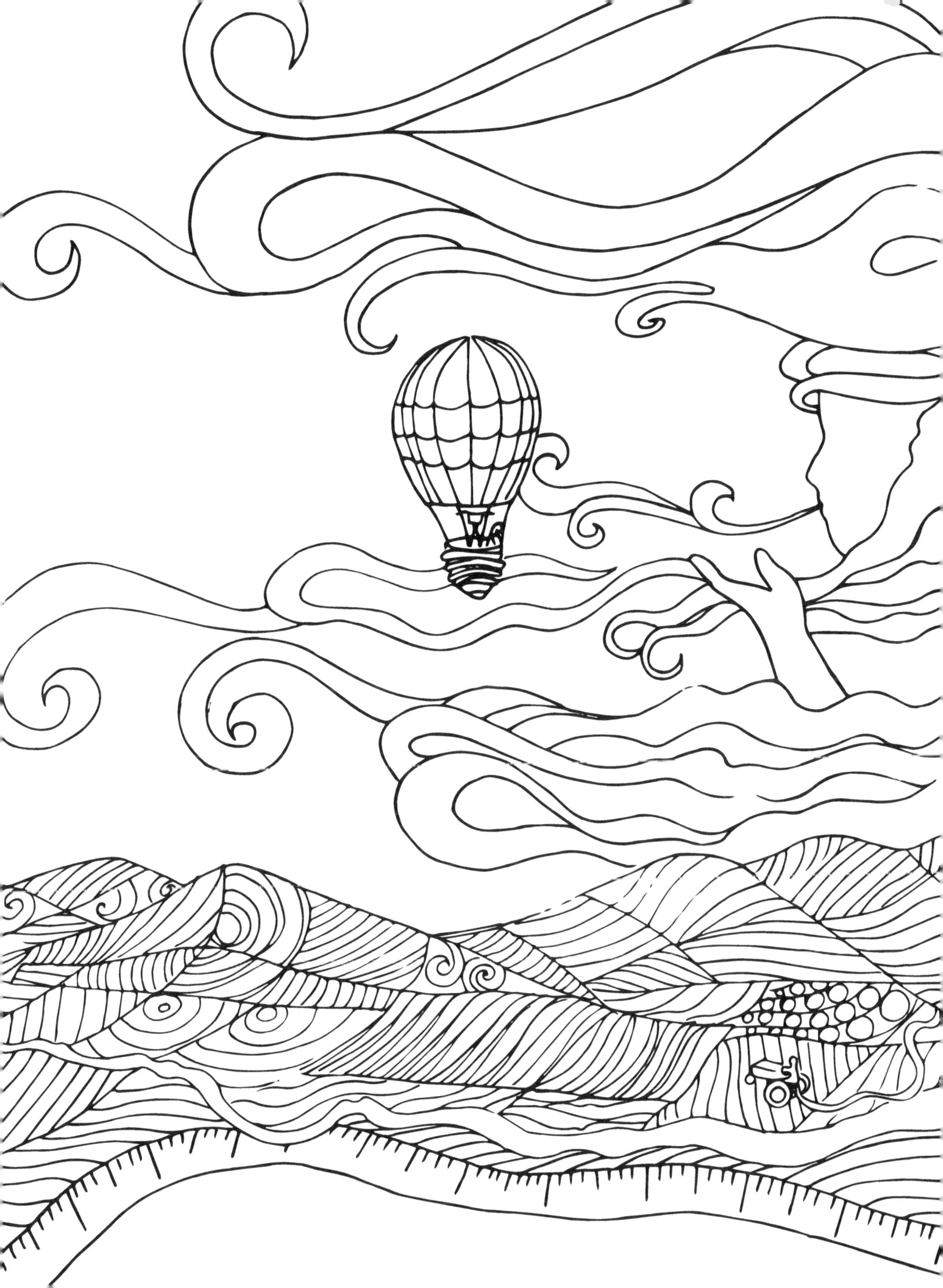

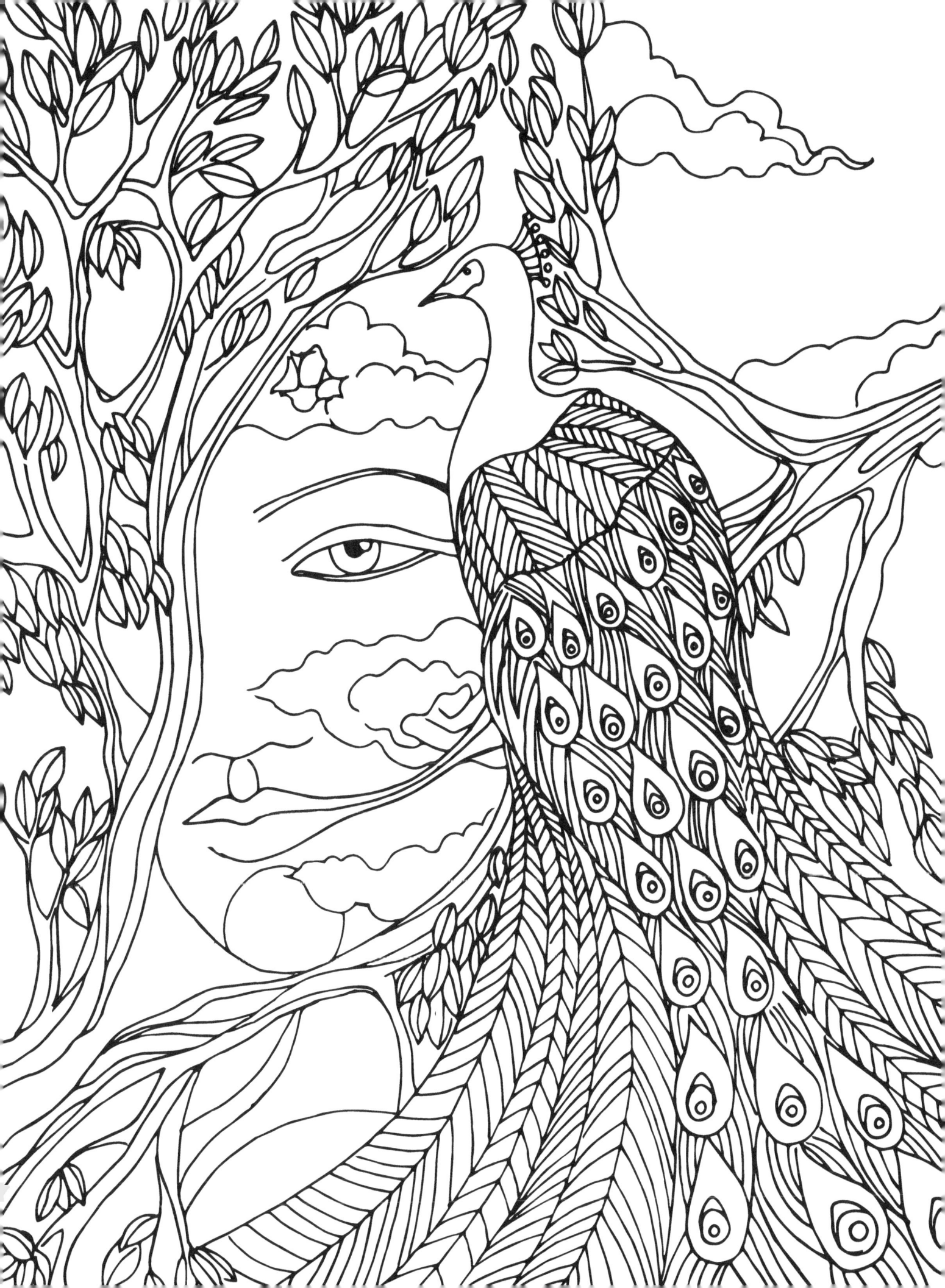

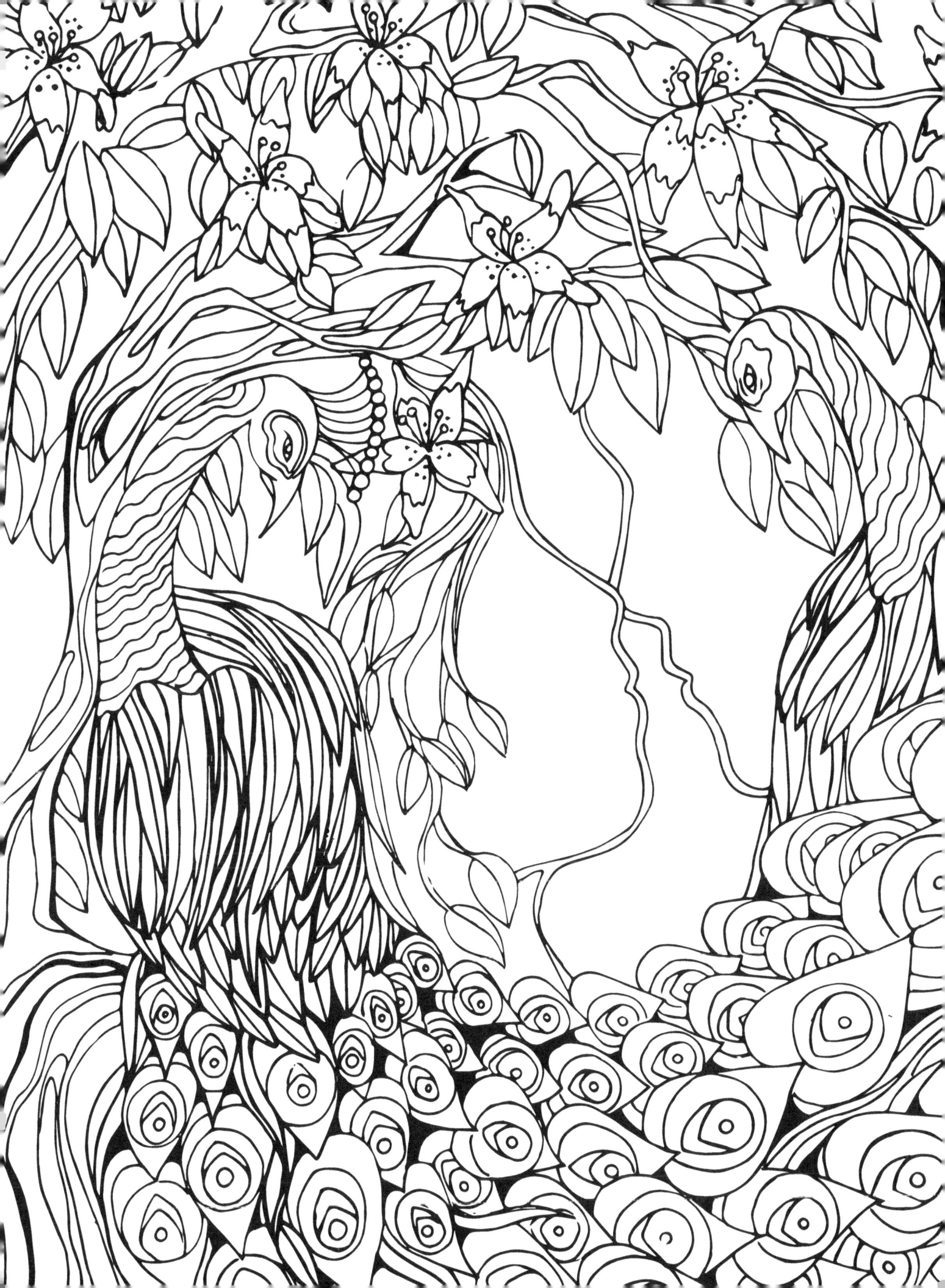

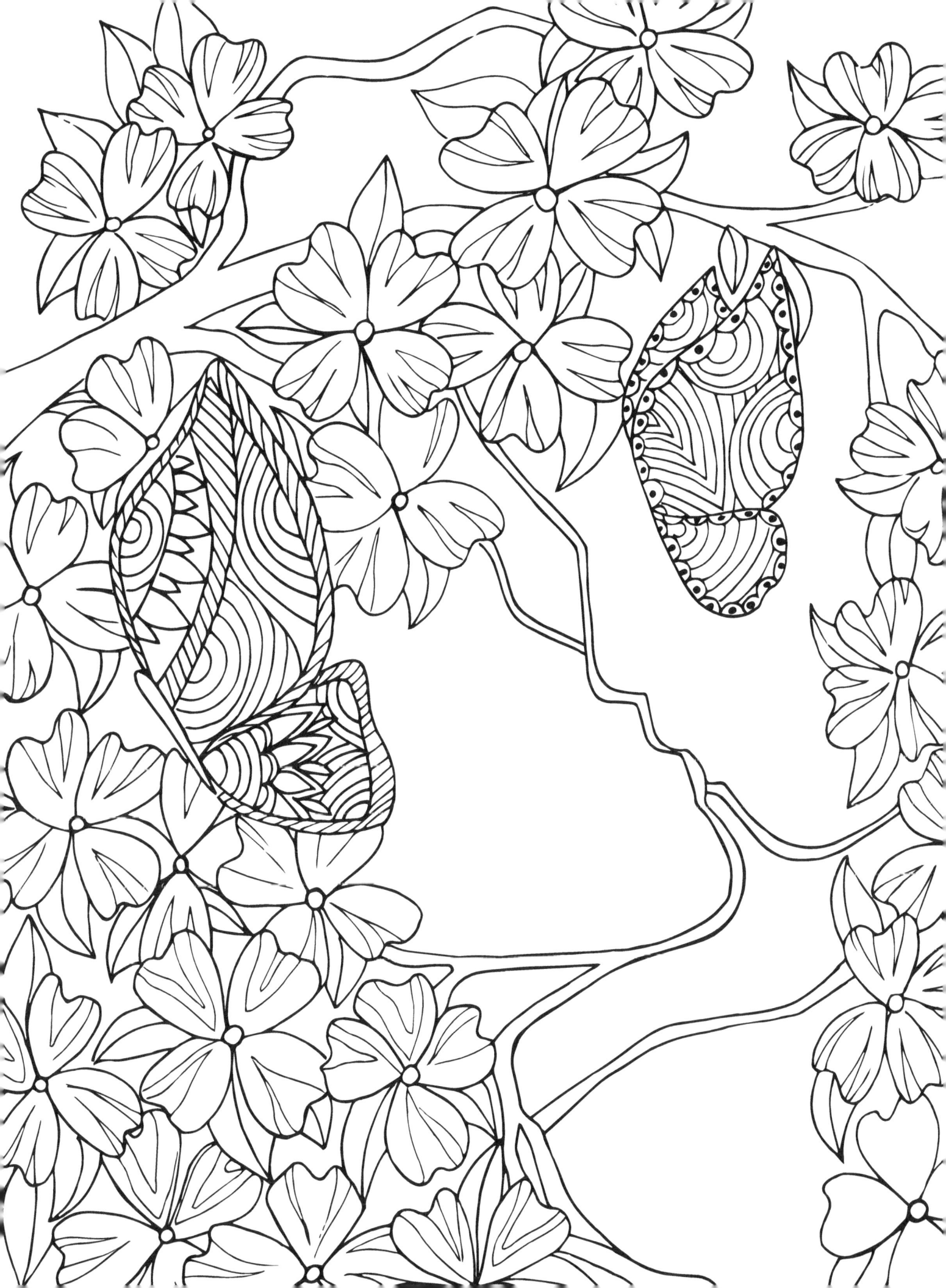

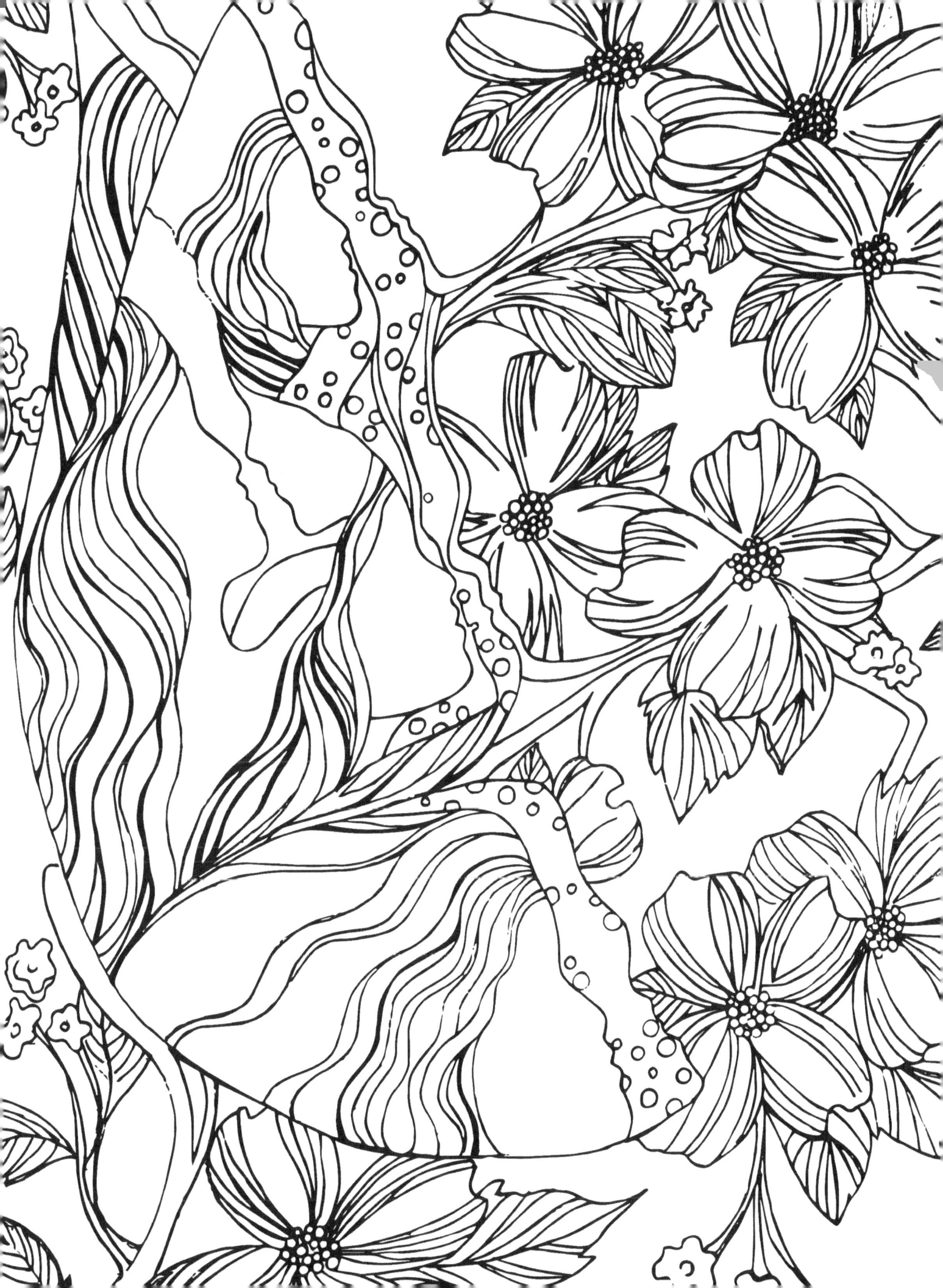

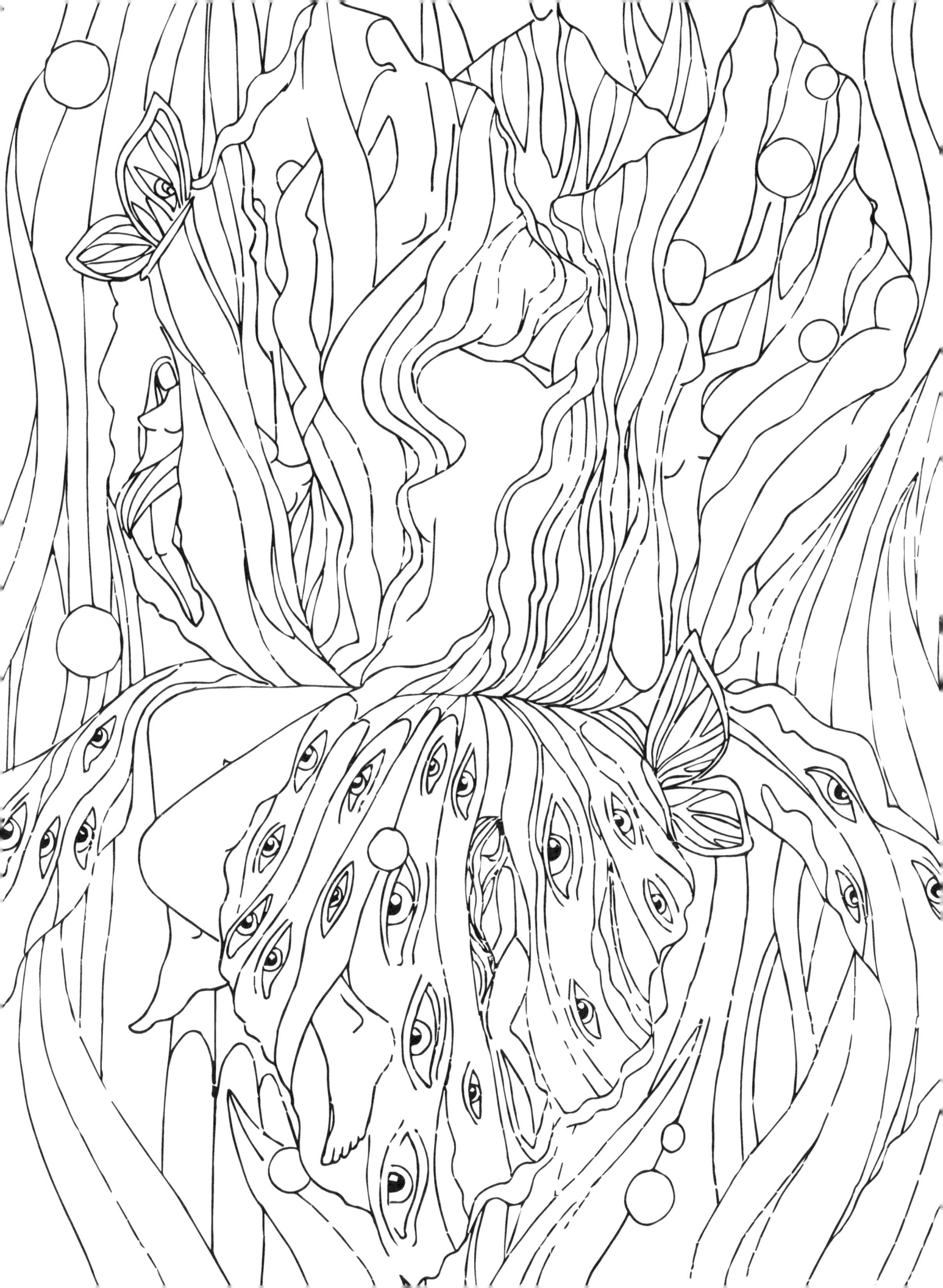

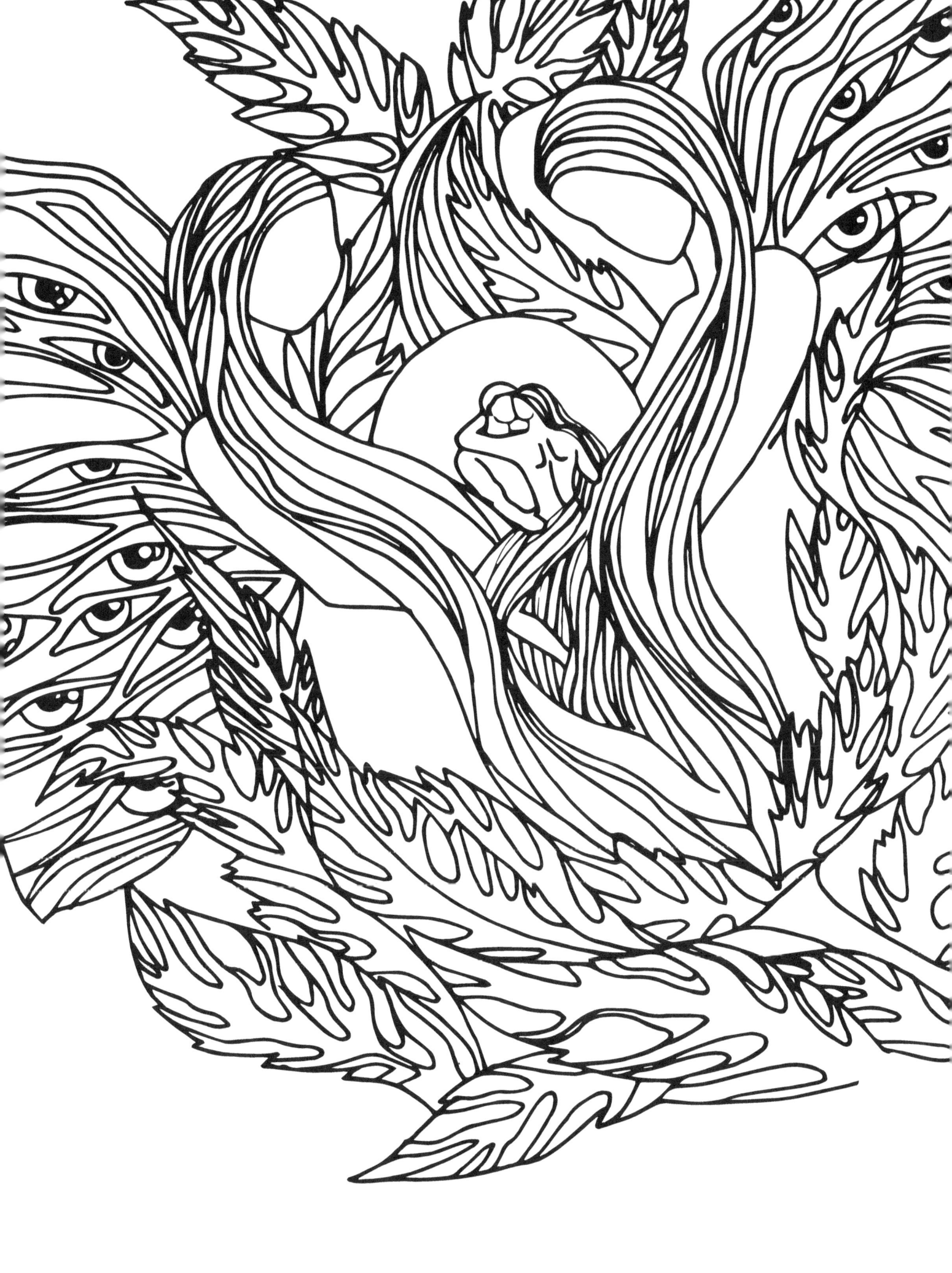

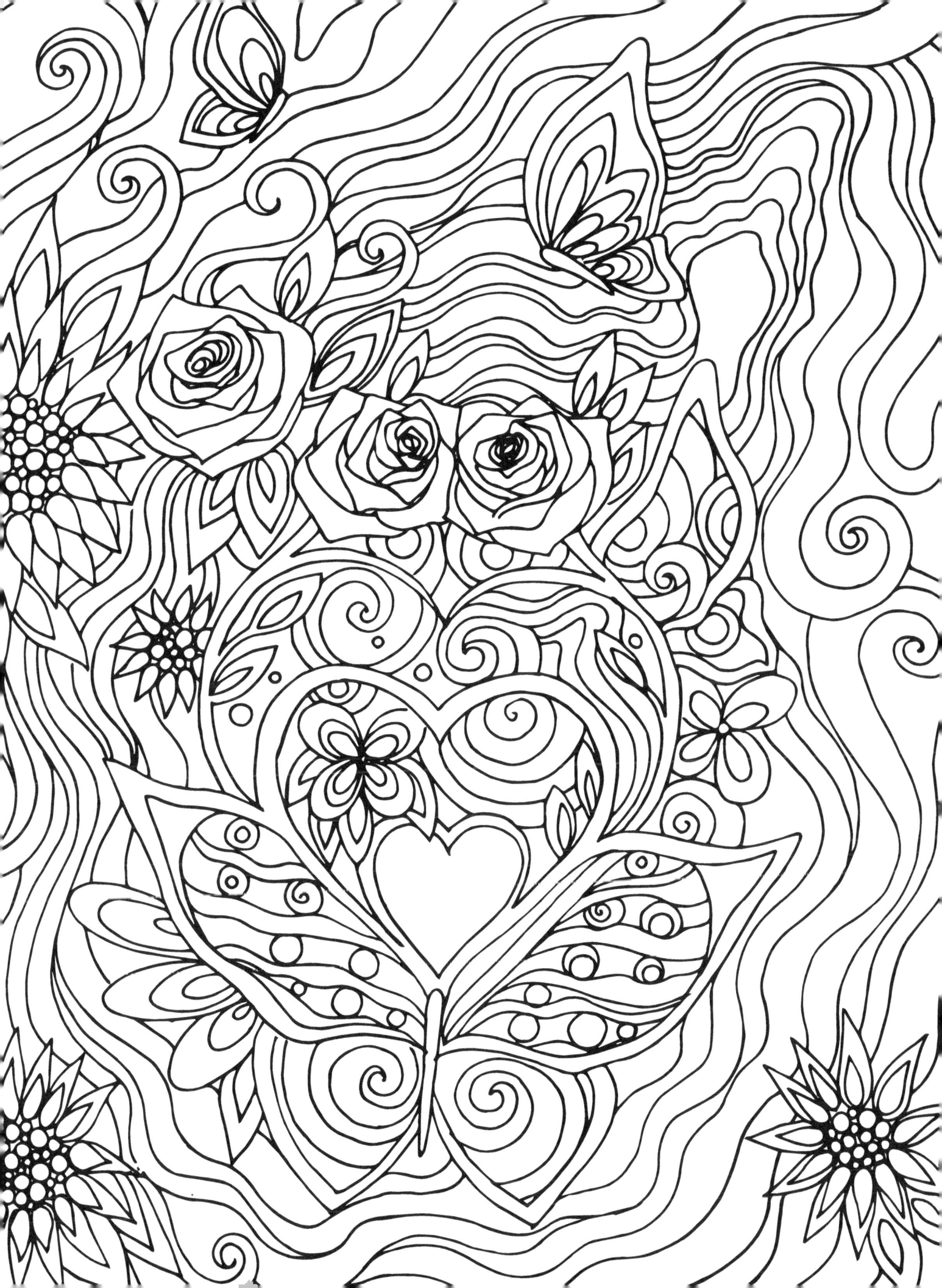

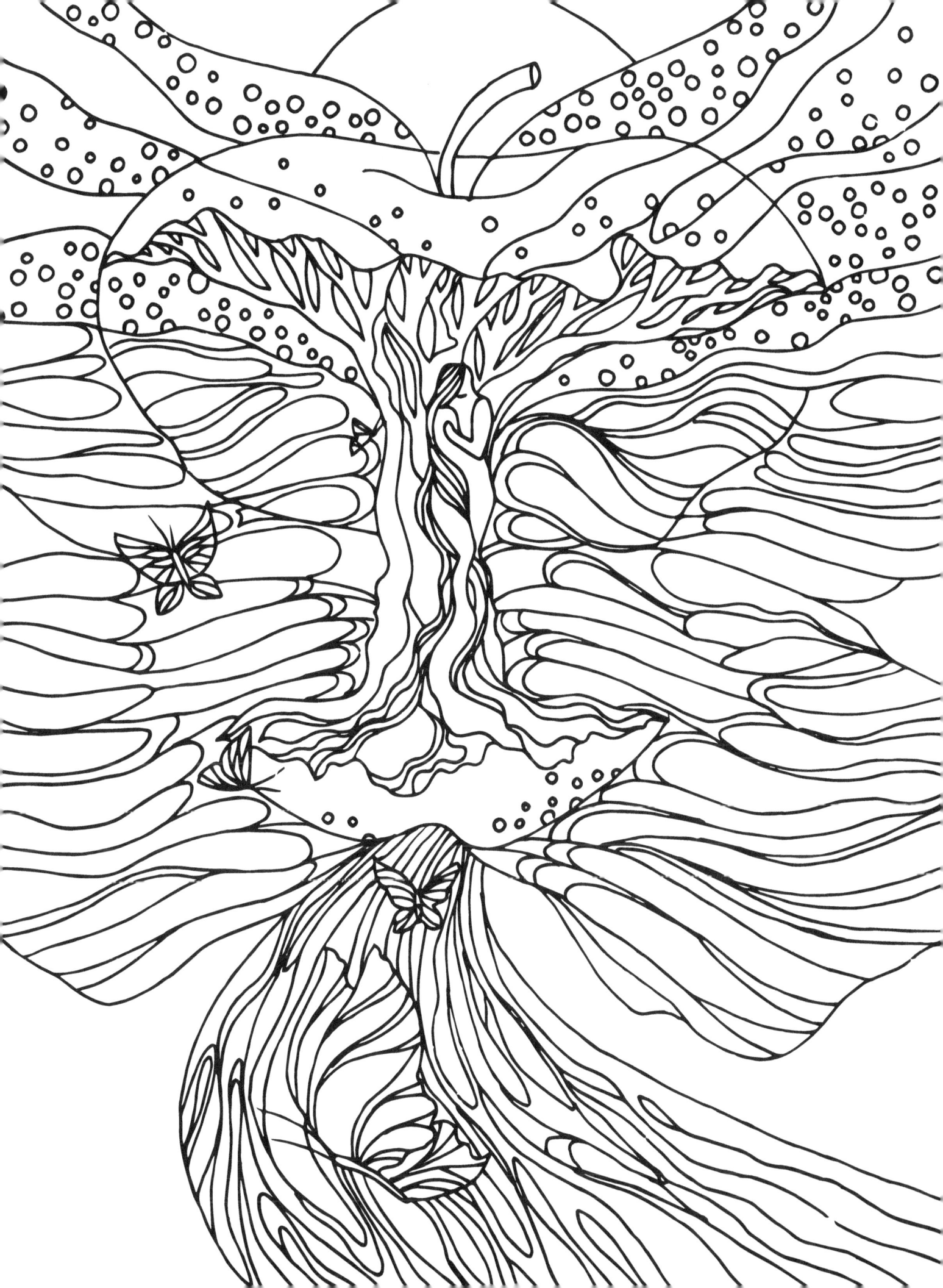

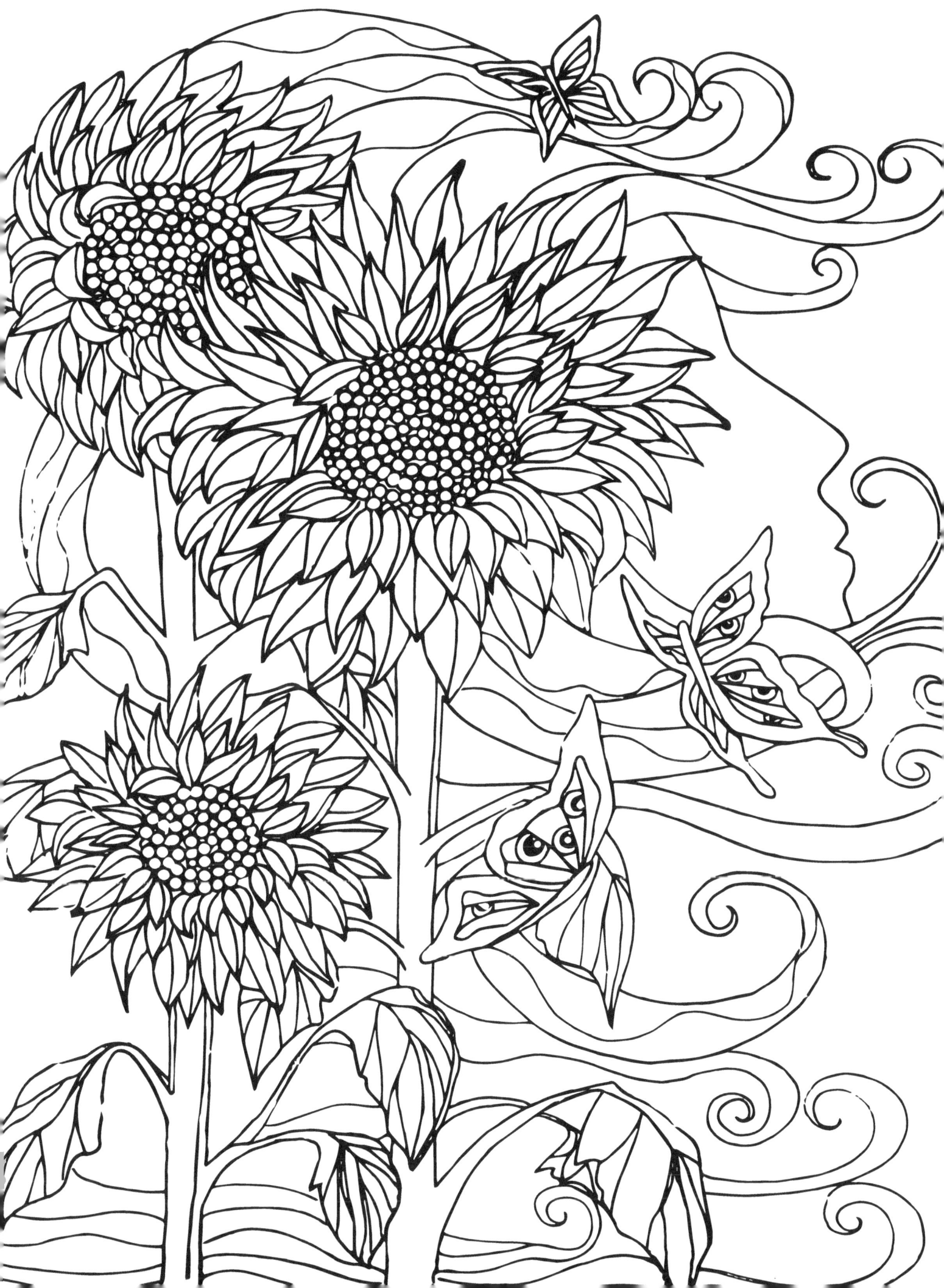

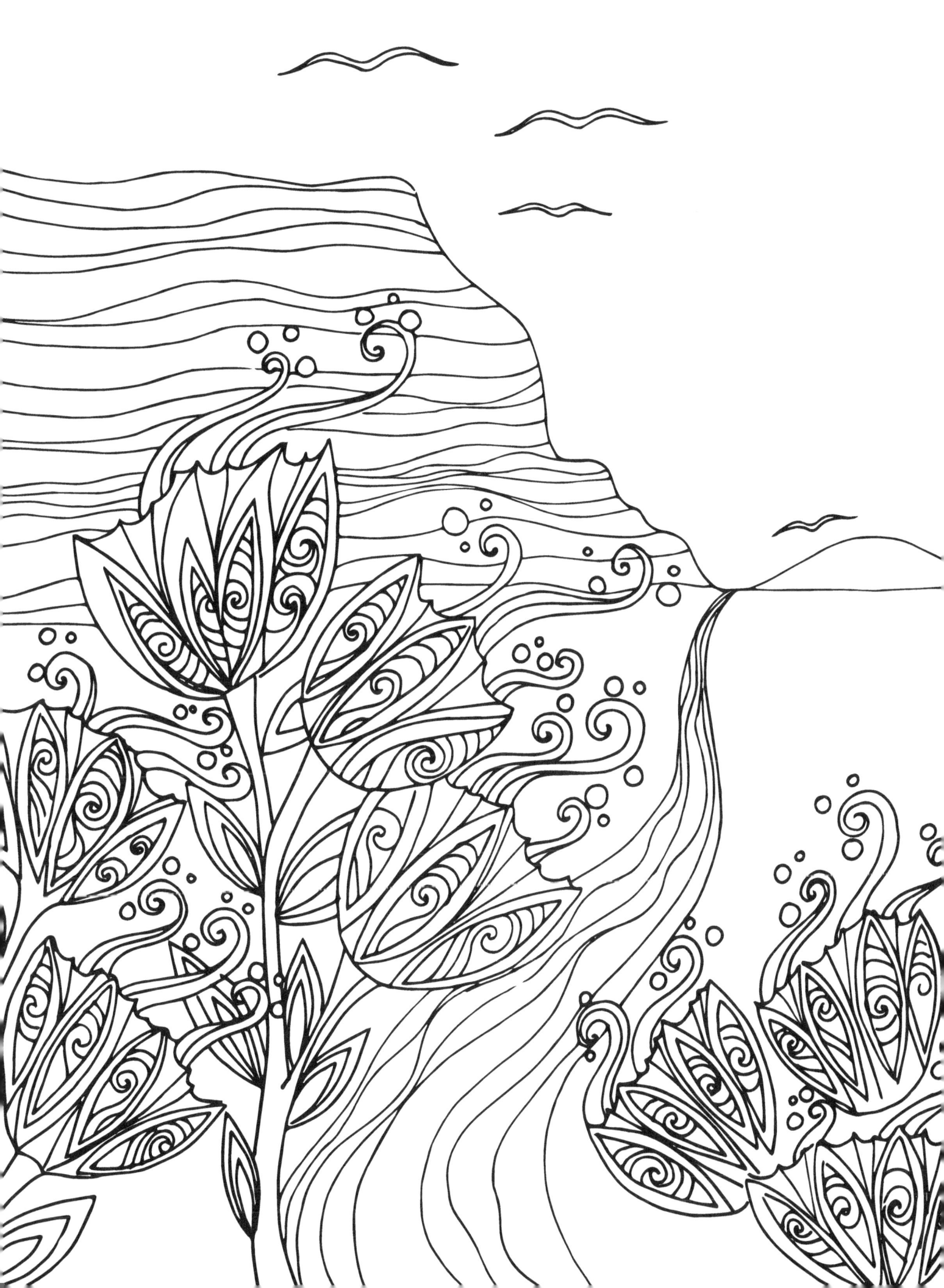

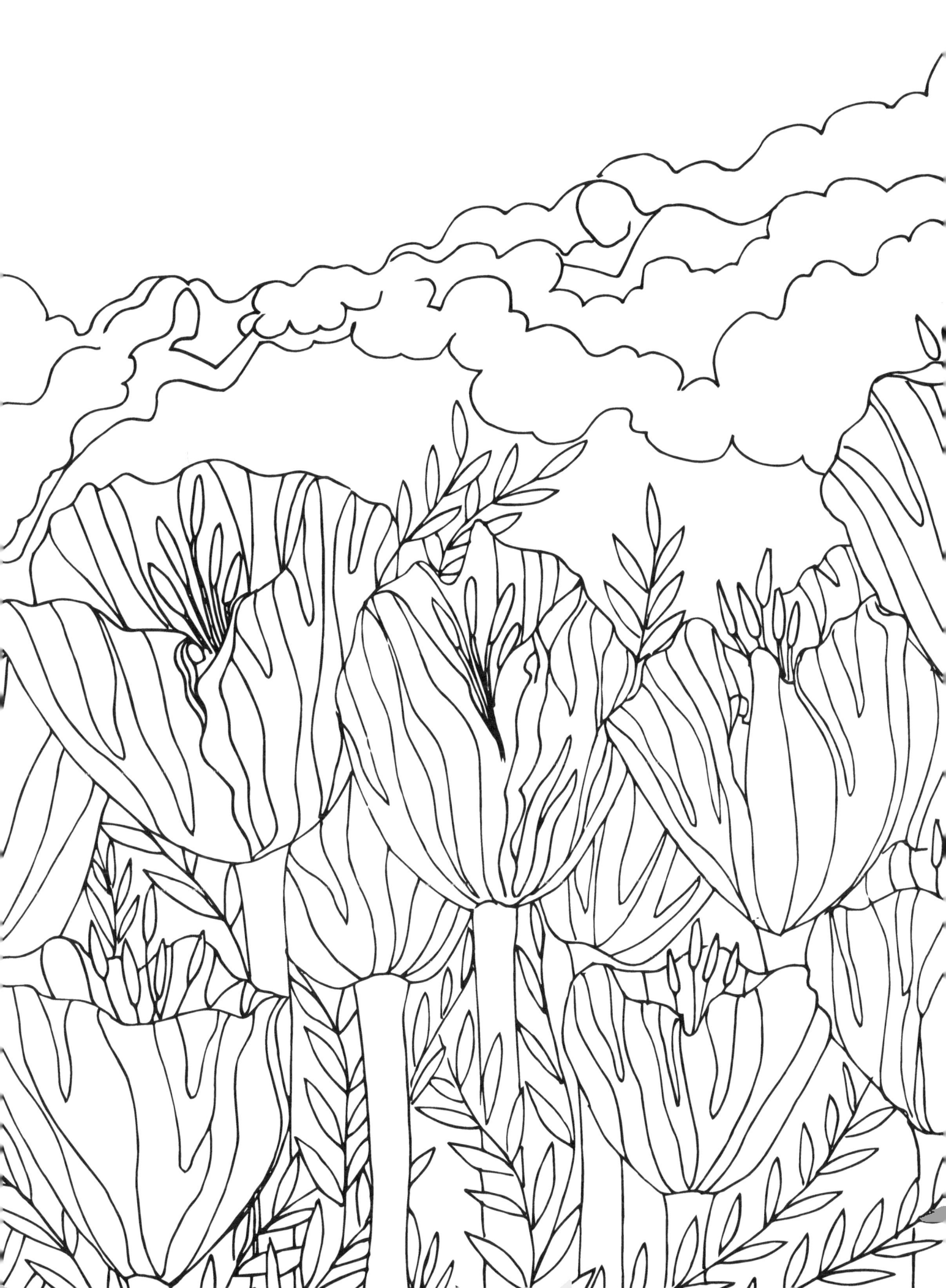

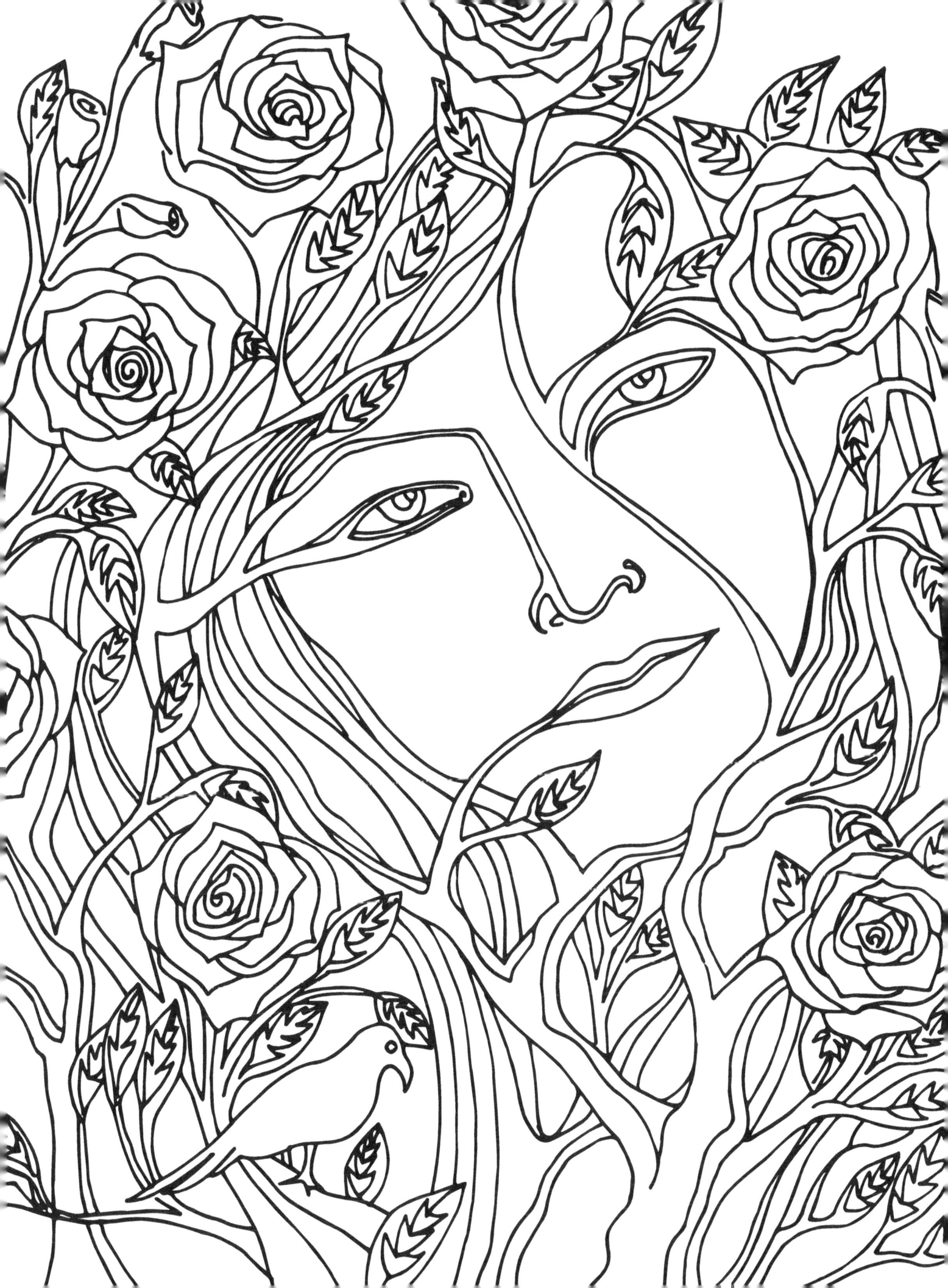

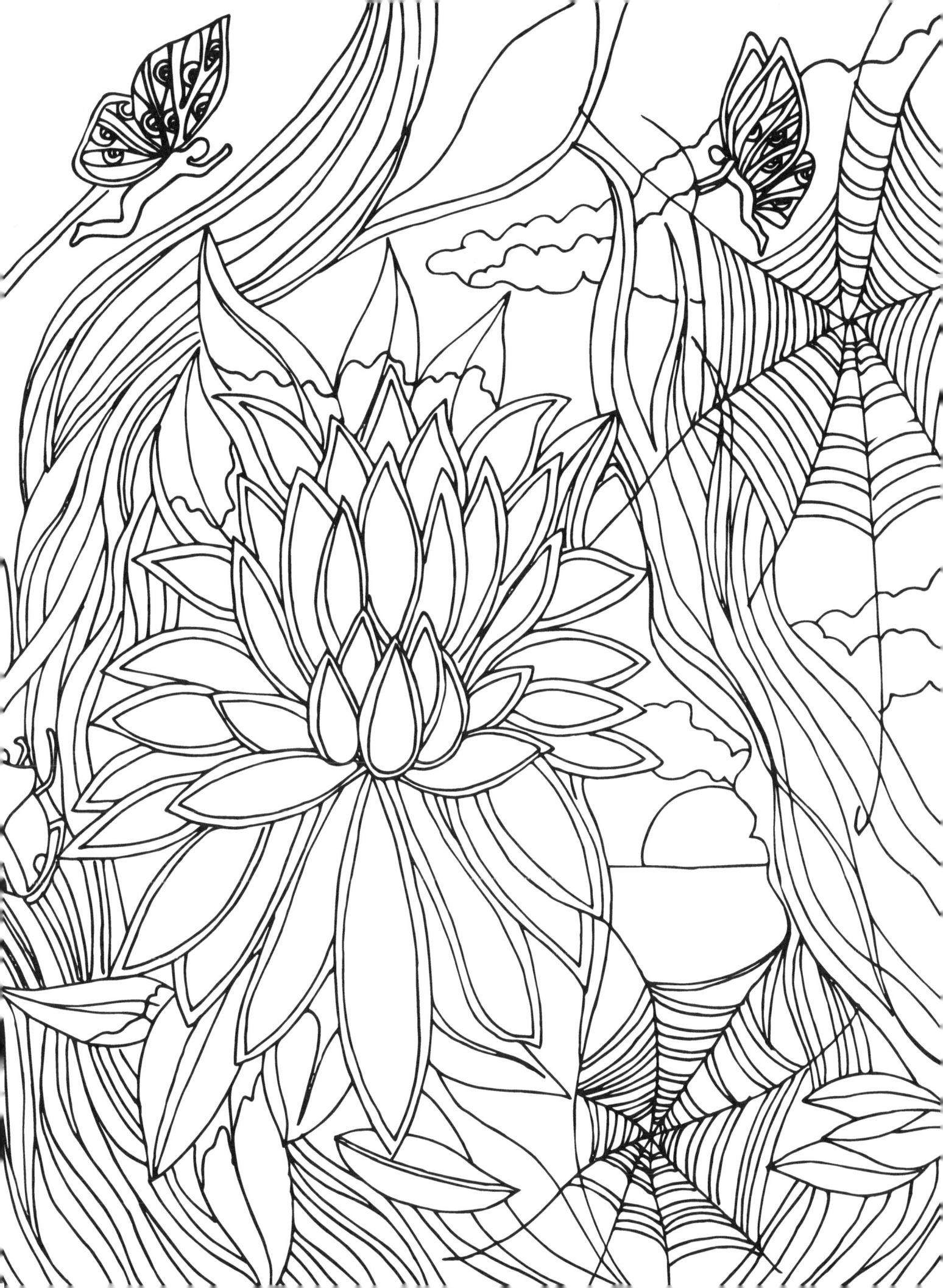

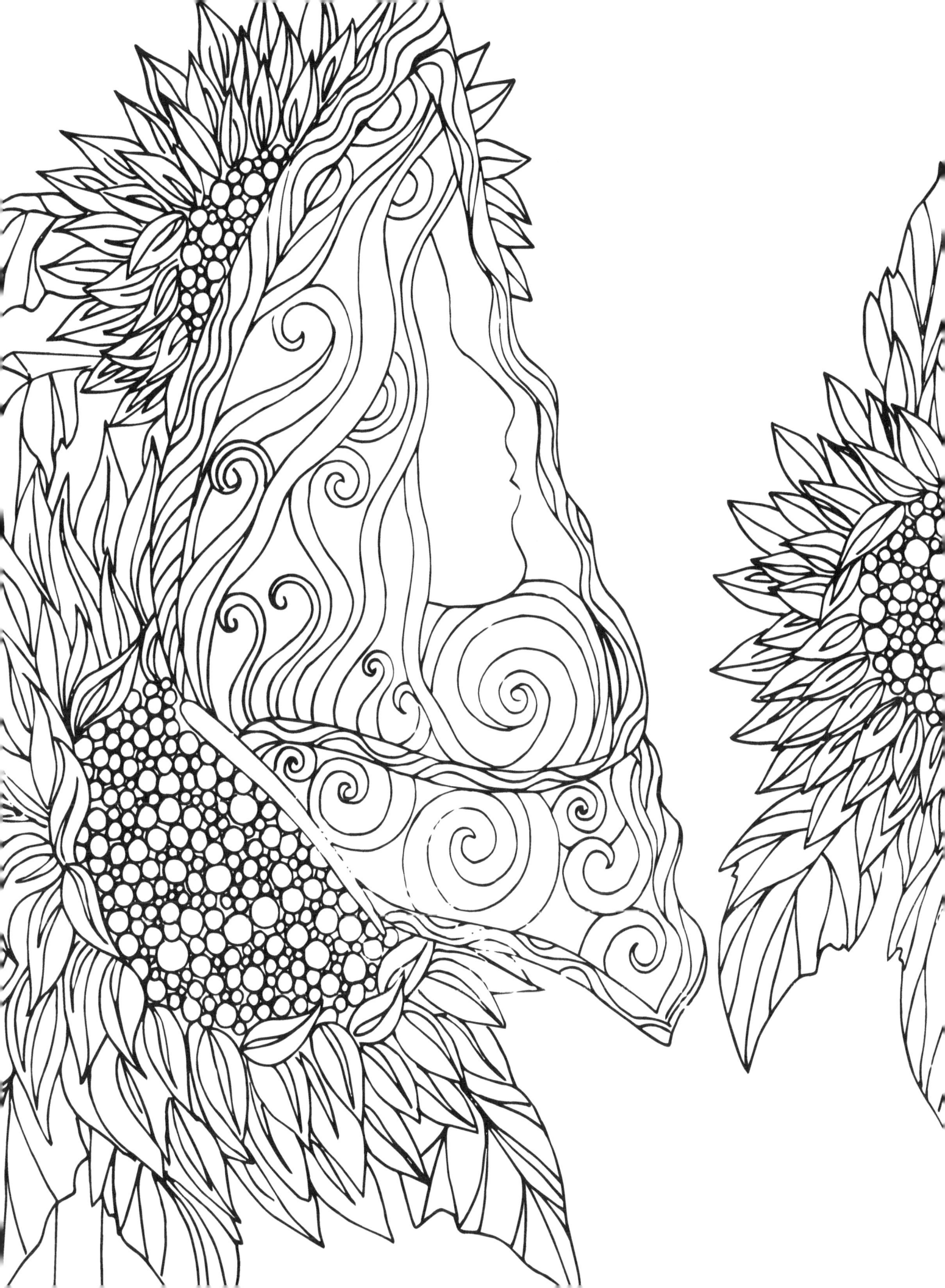

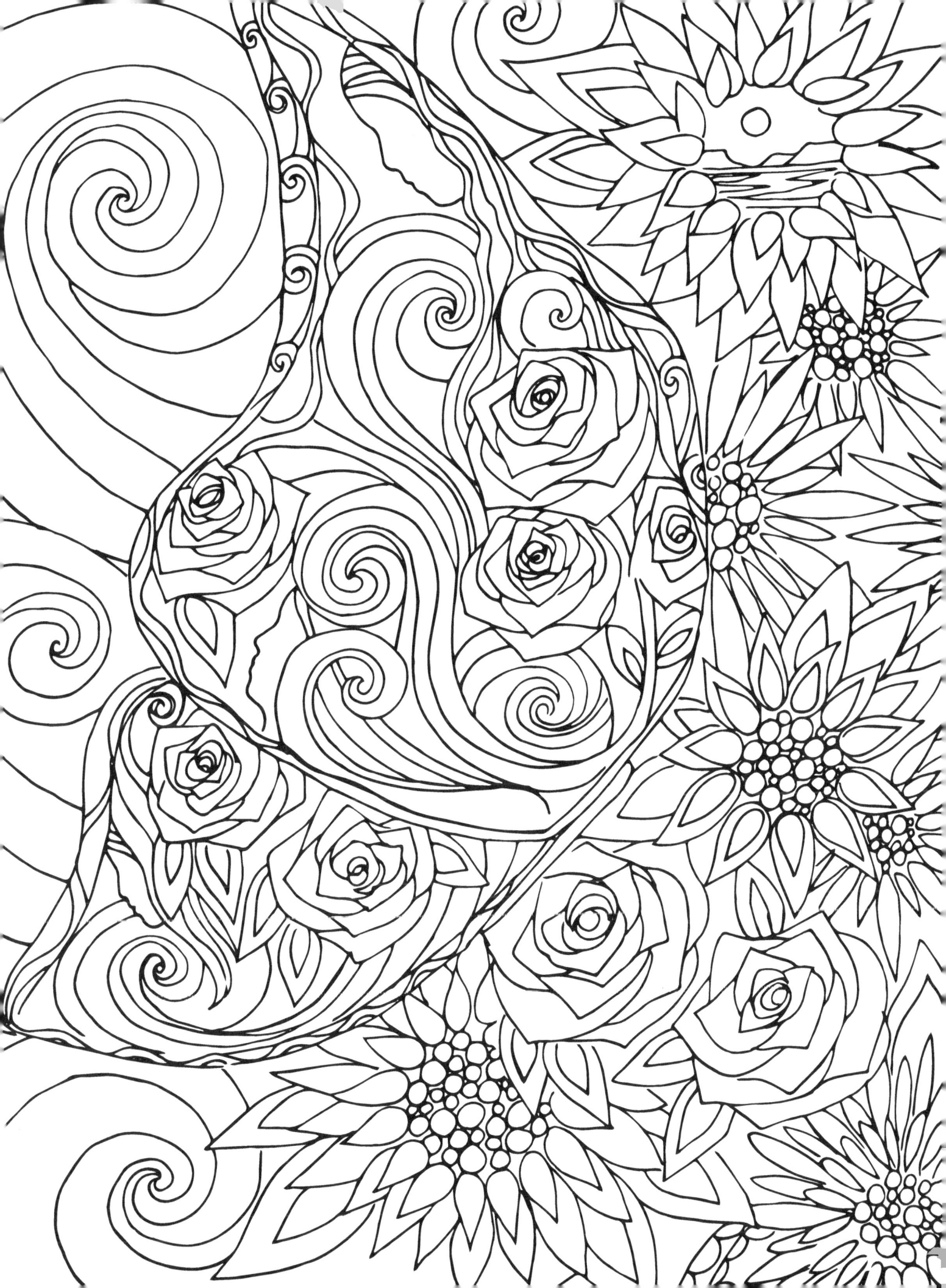

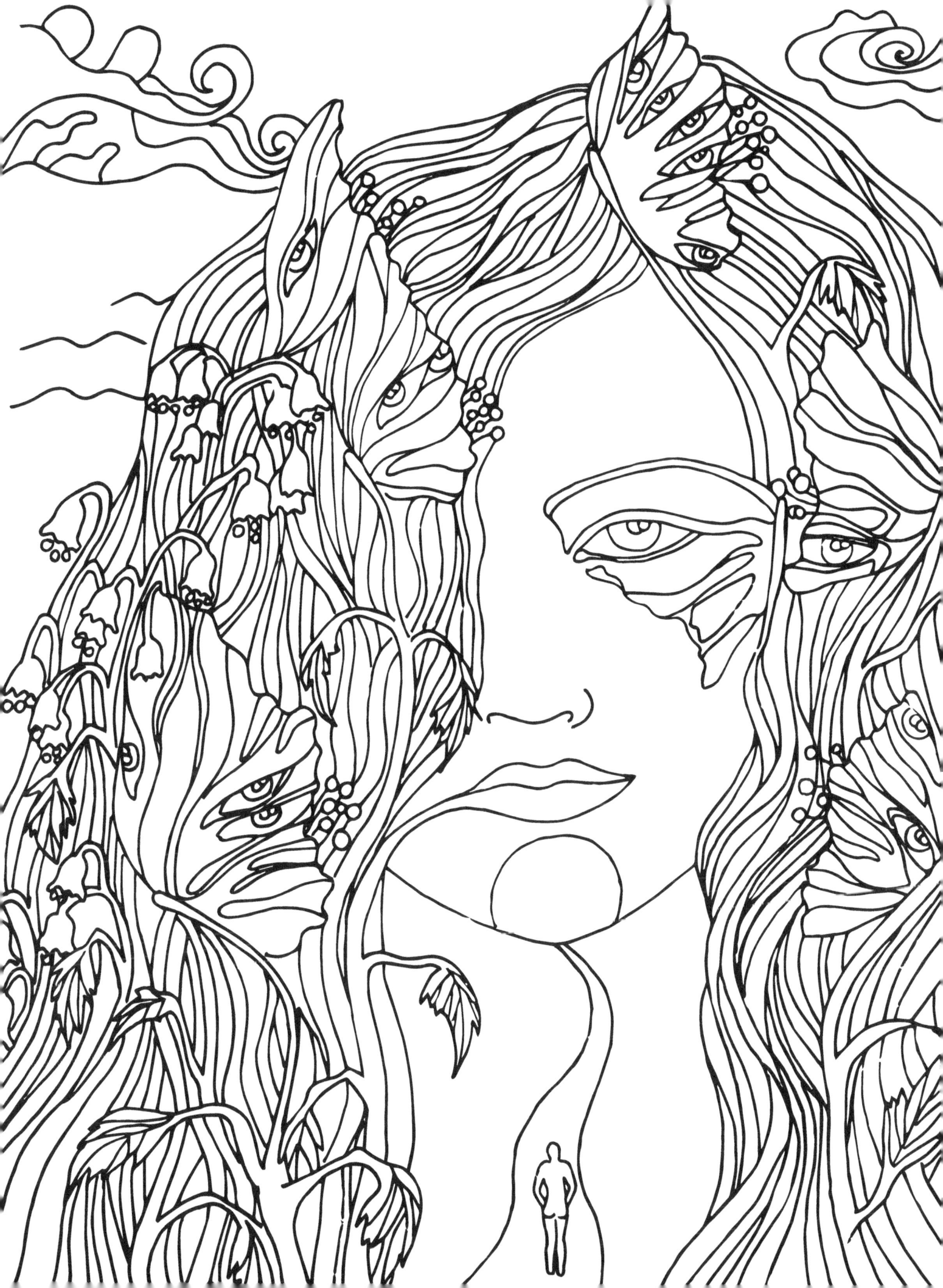

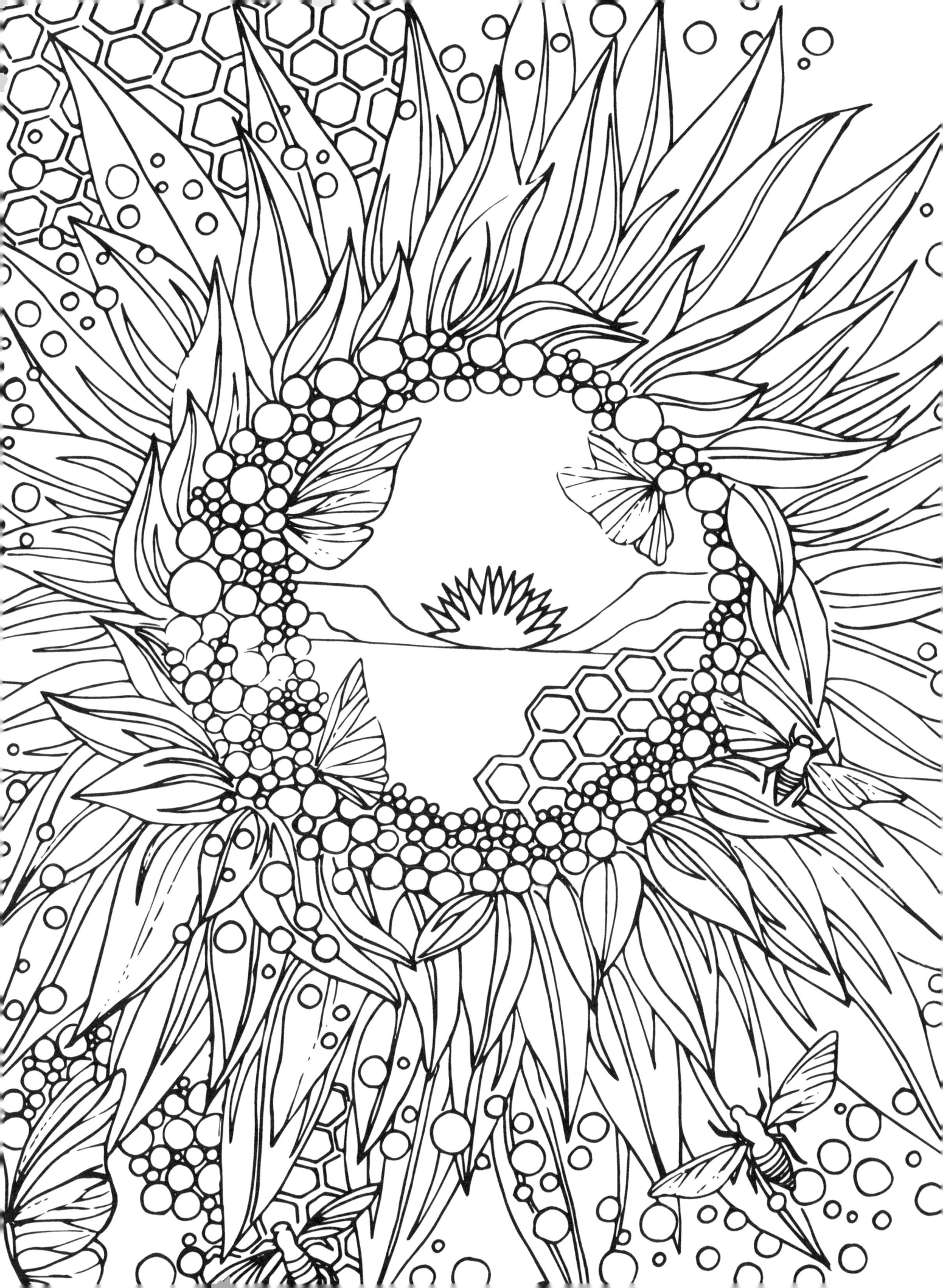

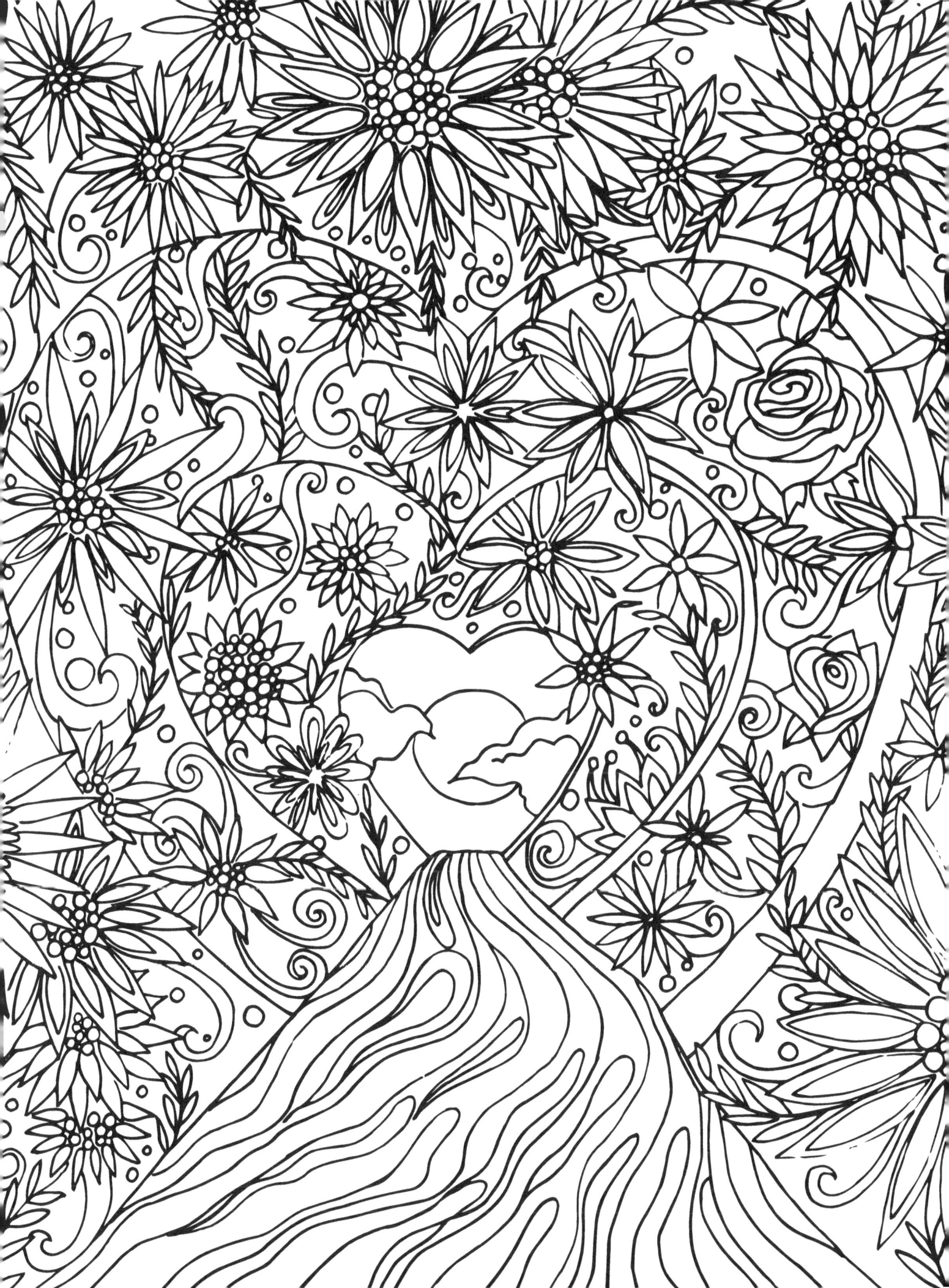